Think Like A BRAND

A **7**-Step Strategic Brand Plan™
To Increase Your Career Satisfaction and Success

By Pamela J. Green,
MBA, SPHR, ACC

ISBN: 978-0-9886804-4-9
First Edition. Printed in the United States of America
Published by: Pamela J. Green Solutions, LLC, Washington DC
Copyediting by Susan Black
Lead Designer, Erin Davis
Art Direction, Evelyn Davis-Walker, www.daviswalkercreative.com
Cover and back copy photography by Valerie Woody, Photographer, www.valeriewoody.com
Jeff Bezos Photo: "Jeff Bezos' iconic laugh" by Steve Jurvetson - Flickr: Bezos' Iconic Laugh. Licensed under CC BY 2.0 via Commons - https://commons.wikimedia.org/wiki/File:Jeff_Bezos%27_iconic_laugh.jpg#/media/File:Jeff_Bezos%27_iconic_laugh.jpg
Sara Blakely Photo: "Sara Blakely" by Gillian Zoe Segal - Self-photographed. Licensed under CC BY-SA 4.0 via Wikimedia Commons - https://commons.wikimedia.org/wiki/File:Sara_Blakely.jpg#/media/File:Sara_Blakely.jpg
Misty Copeland Photo: Sam Aronov / Shutterstock.com
Steve Harvey Photo: "SteveHarveyHWOFMay2013" by Angela George. Licensed under CC BY-SA 3.0 via Commons - https://commons.wikimedia.org/wiki/File:SteveHarveyHWOFMay2013.jpg#/media/File:SteveHarveyHWOFMay2013.jpg
Beyonce Knowles Photo: Kevin Winter / EdStock / iStock Photo
Michael Strahan Photo: JStone / Shutterstock.com
Taylor Swift Photo: Jason Merritt / EdStock / iStock Photo

Mom and Dad:

For the press of your hand in my back gently pushing me forward....
thank you.

PREFACE

Do you ever:
- Feel overlooked, underappreciated, and undervalued?
- Feel long on frustration, short on career options?
- Look back on missed job opportunities with regret?
- Struggle with what to do next?
- Want more success, but aren't sure how to turn your goals into reality?
- Want to bring your contributions to the attention of your supervisor?

Did you know:
According to research by OI Global Partners, there are two significant reasons people are not getting the jobs and enjoying the careers they desire most:

- They do not sufficiently differentiate themselves from others (selected by 67% of career consultants)
- They fail to successfully transfer past experiences to the current job opportunity (64%)

Additionally, according to the *Gallup State of the Global Workplace Report*, they found that most disengaged workers globally are "checked out" and "sleepwalking through their day."

Don't check out, grab the job of your dreams! Don't sleepwalk thru years of a career, do what you love! Take a bold approach and disrupt your traditional career path! Sure, you can innovate your career, transform what you have into something better, but usually this maintains a consistent path. Disruption will move you to an entirely new playing field.

For example, innovative steps in a Marketing career as an Assistant can move you into another Marketing role to pull on your marketing experience. That is good, safe and pretty traditional. We've taken these gradual steps for hundreds of years, and this path can certainly send you sailing into retirement.

However, disrupting your career, deviates from the traditional approach and paves new customized paths to success. This approach is exciting and rewarding because it pulls on all of your talents, not just a few.

I didn't want to waste my career potential. And I certainly didn't want to waste time going down a path that did little to help me explore all that I could offer, or that did not fully leverage all of my talent. So I learned how to borrow success strategies from the best and the brightest disruptors in sports, entertainment, business and the arts to build a scalable career plan that is strategic, congruent with my organization's goals and would lead me to the success I desire – and so can you!

What we are embarking on is more than creating an outline or finding your strengths — you are going to create a unique template that pushes you to use your strengths to differentiate your brand from others!

I'm offering you a first-of-a-kind approach that gives you more control over your career success. A plan to shift your approach to success that breaks with conformity, that positions you for the type of career and career options you never thought possible – a **7-Step Strategic Brand Plan™** to disrupt your traditional career path and set you on a customized path to success.

Why me?

Three years ago I was an executive for a large global organization. I was traveling 70% of the time. I was putting in 60 hours a week. I was managing a local team and a virtual team. I was responsible for millions of dollars in revenue. I was making a lot of money, and I was exhausted.

I woke up one day and thought to myself, "Is this success?" On the one hand, I was celebrated for my talent and on the other hand, I was resented, marginalized, and undervalued. I told myself, "Enough! Something's got to change. If I'm going to work this hard for someone else, I might as well get something more fulfilling out of the opportunity". It was then and there that I began to work on my Brand Plan.

Now a few years later, I'm happy to say that I still have a boss – many of them. But while I help them achieve their goals, I too, get to achieve mine. I get to work for clients who thrill me and appreciate my talent. I get to travel all over the world, doing what I love without restraint, feeling that my contributions really matter – everyone wins!

This is why I am so excited to share what I've learned with you - so you don't have to do it alone. So you don't have to look back on your career after 10, 20, or 30 years and say "Why didn't someone tell me about this years ago?" In retrospect, I'm glad it all happened. I'm so thankful for the wonderful experiences I had but also thankful for some of the worst experiences of my professional career. Were it not for those combined experiences, I wouldn't have the **7-Step Strategic Brand Plan™** to share with you today.

Why this topic?

Look at Steve Harvey, Michael Strahan and Sara Blakely. They are not just sports, business and entertainment celebrities and entrepreneurs, they are brands. Brands that disrupted the conventional path they were on, built on their talents to broaden their career options, and now enjoy unconventional career success.

Michael Strahan is a wonderful example of someone who took his skills playing for the NY Giants on the field and successfully converted them to off the field talent. Look at how many athletes go bankrupt - according to Sports Illustrated, 78% of NFL players face bankruptcy within two years of leaving the game! Michael read the reports and took immediate action to disrupt that path in exchange for one that not only broke with tradition, but that would expose his other talent. He didn't wait until his career was over to think about, and plan for, his next move and neither should you.

I have had my foot in two worlds; as an advocate for employees and as an advocate for organizations. As a business and HR executive, I saw how other sport, entertainment and art talents were thinking and acting like true professional brands, and I realized, I could apply this same strategy to my career. I saw leaders with great talent who didn't know how to leverage their people's talent, and everyone was suffering. I witnessed firsthand how employees were not managing their professional brands. Organizations were getting frustrated and weren't helping them. Nobody was winning.

Thinking like a brand is more than identifying talent, or even having multiple talents; it is about identifying and developing multiple _marketable_ talents that are sought by consumers and that you can leverage in unique ways. Steve Harvey turned his talent for connecting with people and making them laugh into a multi-million dollar "Steve Harvey" brand that includes a talk show, game show, books, movies and other enterprises – all marketable and innovative.

My final point is this: the degree to which your talents are marketable rests not only in the need for your talent but also in how well your personal character can deliver on your brand's promise. Think about the countless number of athletes, actors, and musicians with

> TWEET THIS:
> **"It's time for the #business world to embrace their #multi-talented performers." #careers #leaders #branding #TLAB**

marketable talents whose character made them undesirable. Now, think about those individuals you've worked with in the past, who seemed to
have the technical capability but whose conduct, attitude and behavior could not uphold their brand.

Why you?

You might be thinking, I'm a single parent, my pay is ok, but I'm working lots of hours and I'm focused on getting my kids through school which leaves me little time to think about anything else, let alone _Think Like A Brand_ – how do I really benefit from something like this?

Why you? I asked myself this same question and one day a friend sent me this timely message. I hope it motivates you in the same way:

"Your time is limited, so don't waste it living someone else's life. Don't be trapped by dogma - which is living with the results of other people's thinking. Don't let the noise of other's opinions drown out your own inner voice. And most important, have the courage to follow your heart and intuition. They somehow already know what you truly want to become. Everything else is secondary."

Steve Jobs, Entrepreneur

When we finally realize that our talent is a seed to be sown, we can stop wasting our lives living someone else's. We find the time to identify new ways to grow our value, our options and our professional longevity. I was working tons of hours, and I finally realized there was STILL much more to my talent than what was being leveraged and sown into the world so I made the time to invest in my future not just for me but for my family too!

> TWEET THIS:
> **"Your time is limited, so don't waste it living someone else's life." Steve Jobs #careers #branding #TLAB**

You're about to learn a unique approach to identify, develop and leverage your skills into marketable talent — an approach that provides you with a competitive edge over other candidates and multiple career choices when you're ready to make a change. The more directly you develop your talents, the more options you have to secure the career you desire. Do you believe you have something more to offer?

Why now?

I know this works. I've personally coached individuals like you who did not think a layoff would happen to them. Individuals who:

- Found themselves backed into a corner at work and feeling out of career options
- Have felt too old to think about branding themselves
- Who simply felt stuck and unsure of what to do next

One individual in particular, was wrestling with the desire to leave his well-paying job, feeling stuck in a slow-moving bureaucratic corporate culture that wasn't leveraging his

> TWEET THIS:
> **"The more directly you develop your talents, the more options you have to secure the career you desire." #careers #talent #branding #TLAB**

talent. I asked him if there were other things he'd like to be doing that his company could support or prepare him for. Through a series of coaching discussions, he identified several related talents that could be leveraged by the organization, and that would offer additional career fulfillment without him having to immediately look for another job. He won, his company won. The shift wasn't bad, it was aligned.

How about this: according to the U. S. Bureau of Labor Statistics, on average some 50,000 people are laid off or discharged from their jobs every day. How many people are professionally prepared for their discharge or layoff? Even if you know in advance, it doesn't mean you are prepared to make important decisions about what you'll do next.

Why now? Because you have to become the caretaker of your own career. I know how HR thinks, and I also know how your boss thinks. When I'm HR, I'm in meetings all day, advocating for people and programs. I simply don't have the bandwidth to look out for each and every person who works in the company. Likewise, as the leader, I'm at a level where I'm trying to be an advocate for the division to move objectives forward so we can achieve our goals. In this role, I'm looking for you to step up and speak up and show me what you've got!

I'll show you how. I'll share a methodology that will teach you how to build your brand borrowing success strategies from talents such as Taylor Swift, Beyoncé, and Jeff Bezos. From them and many others, you will learn how to build a brand full of professional satisfaction and career longevity. What is your level of determination?

Why this way?

What exactly are we seeking to innovate? We are after your mindset - how you think about yourself, your talent, and your approach to your career. As you'll read in the pages of this book, the blueprint has been created by others in sports, entertainment, business and arts. I borrowed from that blueprint and creatively applied it to achieve my goals, and I believe you can too.

Form follows function, meaning the shape of a thing should be based upon its intended function or purpose. A building is designed to fit its intended purpose. You were designed for an intended purpose and all of your training, skills and experiences are coming together for this moment in time.

The **7-Step Strategic Brand Plan**™ works for those willing to apply themselves, those unwilling to relent to the traditional way of pursuing their careers. It works for companies willing to change

> "It's a shame when people allow themselves to get all mixed up and permanently set."
>
> **John Maxwell, author**

how they view and engage talent, and it works for people who are serious about taking control of their careers.

Isn't this about *building* a strength? No, this is about *teaming* all of your strengths so there is balance and a collective value. A strength means you have the potential to be good at something. A talent is something you've developed and made marketable. You'll learn from real life examples of people who've identified and leveraged their strengths and talents in ways that have given them the value, options and professional longevity they are looking for. Does your form follow your function?

My Promise.

I know you're busy, so I'm going to present you with strategies that are easy to understand and adopt. No ivory tower stories, but instead real, down to earth examples. I will challenge the traditional way in which you are managing your career, and then I'll provide you with an easy to follow strategy for becoming a cross-capable brand - a brand capable of making many contributions, sometimes in different but related areas of your performance.

I'm going to make it easy for you to identify your transferable skills. I'm going to teach you how to identify an organization's brand, needs and priorities so that your brand is delivering what you want and what your organization needs. As you'll discover, while you grow your visibility, your success is directly related to the degree to which you fulfill your organization's goals.

FOREWORD

I'll always remember that day, early in my career.

At the end of a Monday morning meeting discussing the week's priorities, I brought up a topic that had been on my mind for months. I told my boss, "I think I deserve a raise!"

She smiled and said, "You're right, you do. I was wondering when you were going to have the courage to come in and ask for it."

Lesson learned. I will always be grateful to her for opening my eyes to the fact that it was MY responsibility to ask for what I felt I deserved, instead of waiting for my boss to give it to me.

Please understand, I had been on the verge of quitting. I had been working long hours, creating fresh programs that were attracting new customers, and making the organization a lot of money.

I kept waiting for my boss to call me into her office and give me a pat on the back, a raise, a promotion, something! Nothing. I felt I was being taken advantage of and was on the verge of leaving this job, even though I loved what I was doing.

Thanks to her, I learned it was my responsibility to speak up on my own behalf, instead of waiting for the recognition, salary and career opportunities I wanted, needed and deserved.

Does any of this sound familiar?

If so, you'll benefit from this book. Pamela shares real-world stories about how she learned, (often, the hard way), that talent, smarts, quality work, and being a team player are important, but they're not enough for you to succeed at the level you deserve. You'll discover how to:

- Define what you want to be known for
- Give decision-makers an opportunity to see you in action doing what you're good at
- Ask for and act on advice from mentors, sponsors and supervisors
- Speak up at meetings with solutions (not problems) so people value what you have to offer
- Be proactive in positioning yourself for your ideal career opportunities
- Love what you do so people want to work with you, for you and around you

Perhaps best of all, Pamela shares step-by-step advice on specific actions you can take to be appreciated, recognized and rewarded for your contributions. Get out your pen and be prepared to take notes. Or, if you're reading this book online, get ready to highlight the "I didn't know that" insights you plan to apply to make a tangible difference in your career success and satisfaction.

Read it and reap.

Sam Horn, Author of *Tongue Fu!*, *POP!* and *Got Your Attention?*

11

TABLE OF CONTENTS

ACKNOWLEDGEMENTS

"Ray, I quote you in this book not because you are my husband but because you are a brilliant man, and the whole world needs to know who you are."

This book is only possible due to the unconditional love, support and words of encouragement from my husband, Ray, and my son, Joshua, who say all the right things just when I need to hear them most. It is for you, Josh that I strive to pave a path worth following. To my friends Susan Black and Evelyn Davis thanks for allowing me to tap your expertise to make this book a reality. To my Cresthill Baptist Church family and Facebook friends, your encouragement takes my breath away. To Sam Horn, your friendship and coaching are inspirational, and your expertise in positioning and messaging is unmatched by any other! To all of those leaders whose paths I have crossed throughout my life, thank you. Every experience with you shapes my today and informs my tomorrow. Finally, thank you to all of my friends and confidants who over the years have provided their shoulder during times of intense development and who are always there to cheer me towards success. For all of you I am eternally grateful.

Pamela

What do we mean by a personal brand?

Why is building a personal brand for yourself important? According to brand strategist and noted author Laura Ries in a Forbes online article, a brand is "a name that stands for something in prospects' minds." Just as Disney's brand stands for "great family fun," history-making African-American female American Ballet Theatre soloist Misty Copeland's brand stands for grace, resilience, strength, and endurance. Your prospects are those decision-makers you encounter daily. Does your brand stand for something in their minds? If so, what? And are you satisfied with that vision of you in their minds?

If you want the opportunity to do the kind of work you enjoy, you'll have to build a personal brand that stands for something and showcase it in a way that helps decision-makers see you the way you want to be seen. A brand viewed as capable, credible and competent can lead to success in your personal life, your volunteer life and especially in your professional life. Here are some definitions that will guide and inform your understanding as we build your personal brand together:

Personal Brand:

Your brand is the emotional promise of a professional experience people have as a result of interacting with you. It is the external expression of the things you do well -- and not so well. A positive experience with your brand can lead to limitless possibilities. The greater the degree your brand is viewed as capable, credible, and competent, the greater your chances of sustainable brand achievement.

> TWEET THIS:
> "Your #brand is the emotional promise of the experience people have when they interact with you. What's your promise?" #careers #TLAB

Scalable Brand:

A scalable brand is sustainable because it has at least three marketable transferable talents that lead to increased professional value, career options and occupational longevity. Talent that is aligned with organizational needs is what builds branding sustainability especially when reinforced by consistent high performance in the minds of decision-makers. When your brand is scalable someone will always need and look for the talent you have developed and are willing to share.

Branding Defined:

Branding is how you market and present yourself. It is getting people to see and embrace you the way you want to be seen and embraced and it reinforces your value. Branding helps shape a decision maker's impression about your "fit" at varying levels and degrees in an organization.

Talent Defined:

Your talent is your cognitive, technical and interpersonal ability to positively demonstrate value through the collective presentation of your skills, strengths, capabilities and aptitudes developed through education, life or work experience.

Transferable Talent Defined:

Transferable talent is the collective presentation of your skills, strengths, capabilities and aptitudes developed through education, life or work experience that you can apply to a variety of career opportunities.

Success Defined:

Success is what we experience when we feel we've accomplished our goals. Having success requires you to have goals. Many have stated they never really feel they experience success - that success is a thing strived for not a thing to be "achieved". We need to embrace and experience success and even some failures, large and small, as they have the power to pave the way to our destiny.

Defining Moments:

A time in which a positive or negative career experience meets an opportunity to make a change that can either advance or impede your success.

Are You Thinking Like A Brand?

Take the Quiz

The first rule in personal branding is to know yourself. You are the owner of your brand, responsible for the development and presentation of your talent. I'm going to show you how to use what you know about yourself and how you work best to discover opportunities that allow you to showcase your strengths in an atmosphere that supports your work style. When this happens, your brand will be received as credible, relevant, and memorable. You will also be able to make a personal connection with your customers, clients, peers, and leaders in a meaningful way that opens the door to the things you want to do in your career, and in your life. So, how well do you know:

"BRAND PERCEPTION IS A BRAND'S REALITY."

Laura Ries, author

Yourself:

(Award yourself one point for each "yes" answer below.)

1. I know the values that drive my personal and career decisions.
2. I know the work that yields the greatest professional success.
3. I know my talents.
4. I know the marketability of my talents.
5. I know how to successfully leverage my talents.

Your Organization:

(Award yourself one point for each "yes" answer below.)

1. I know which industries and/or service areas are in demand for someone with my talent.
2. I know my non-negotiables – those work environments and conditions for which I will not settle.
3. I know what my current leaders need from me.
4. I know the type of leader that brings out the best in me and how to identify that person in an interview.
5. I know what my industry is willing to pay for someone with my talent who demonstrates consistent, congruent results.

Your Organization's Needs:

(Award yourself one point for each "yes" answer below.)

1. I am familiar with the strategic direction of my organization.
2. My goals are aligned with the organization's goals.
3. I am helping my organization leverage my talent.

4. I read, network, and stay on top of industry trends affecting those businesses with the most demand for my talent.
5. I am fairly certain I could foresee how adverse economic, social, political or governmental changes might affect the demand for my talent.

What does it all mean?

15 points = Outstanding work, you are well on your way to Thinking and Acting Like A Brand.

10 points or less = You're on the right track, keep reading, there is work to be done.

Less than 8 points = You're at a foundational point in your career. The only way out is up, and we can help.

Successful sports, entertainment, business and arts celebrities have these three things in common:

1) A talent that is in demand
2) A keen understanding of their primary audience
3) How to satisfy the needs of their primary audience while attracting new supporters

Do you know your audience and their needs? For most of you, your immediate audience is your employer. Your broader audience is made up of those organizations that have need of your talent. They all have specific goals, and they determine whether to financially support your efforts or not. However, it's not all on them. You play a significant role in the satisfaction of your fan, in this case, your employer, and thus the success of your brand.

Success can be short-lived if the brand is not relevant and adaptable, able to have influence in respective industries - ensuring the brand has a broad platform and global appeal. Like celebrity brands we will discuss in this book, in order for your brand to have an enduring and sustainable career, your brand must be scalable. Scalable brands such as Martha Stewart and Oprah Winfrey redefine success to be less about how to stay on the platform that leads to success, but rather how to use the platform to build a brand that influences the behavior, attitude and opinions of others in their favor. This can only happen when you have:

1) A clear sense of self
2) The sagacity to foresee the need to make career shifts that extend the life of your brand
3) An understanding of your organization's brand, needs, and priorities

You see it is so much more than talent alone. Having talent is a start, but I will show you how to apply this same celebrity success blueprint to the management of your personal brand in a way that can lead you to career success. The type of career success and career longevity that you and your organization ultimately desire!

Homework:

a. How do you define success? How does your organization define your success? Are the definitions aligned?

b. Think for a moment about your brand promise. What experience are people having as a result of interacting with you? Do people see you the way you want to be seen? How do you know? Are you satisfied?

c. What are your marketable talents? Are you actively developing them? What other skills do you have that could be expanded and developed?

d. Assess the degree to which your brand is capable, credible, and competent.

how to apply this same celebrity success blueprint to the management of your personal brand in a way that can lead you to career success. The type of career success and career longevity that you and your organization ultimately desire!

WRITE YOUR BRAND STRATEGY

"Success is where preparation and opportunity meet."

Bobby Unser, three-time Indianapolis 500 winner

Michael Strahan

Retired U.S. football defensive end, football hall of famer, football analyst, television co-host, producer, and philanthropist.

"When you're a 20-something-year-old athlete and you're getting a six-figure check every week, you're not thinking about next week. You're not thinking, 'I'm going to be broke,' or 'I'm going to need another job.' But I'll tell you, there are a lot of broke athletes out there - I know plenty - and I didn't want to end up as one."

Michael Strahan

Michael Strahan is a retired U.S. football defensive end who enjoyed a 15-year career with the National Football League (NFL). Michael became a league all-time quarterback sack leader when he set the record for the most sacks in a season in 2001.

Prior to his retirement in 2008, Michael helped his team, the New York Giants, win the 2007 Super Bowl. After retiring from the NFL, Michael found strategic new ways for leveraging his brand that included becoming a football analyst on Fox NFL Sunday and in 2012, serving as the co-host on the television morning show *Live! with Kelly and Michael* alongside Kelly Ripa.

He continues to branch out into television and film, both in front of and behind the camera. His activities also extend into philanthropy. In February 2014, Michael was elected to the Pro Football Hall of Fame. Michael's understanding of brand strategy both on and off the field has led him to an all-around successful career and for these reasons, he epitomizes our first *Think Like A Brand* Secret:

SECRET #1:
Believe in yourself. Be bold - try new things.

"We're our own worst enemy. You doubt yourself more than anybody else ever will. If you can get past that, you can be successful."

Michael Strahan

Strategy can have a mitigating effect on fear. Fear of failure or the fear of ending up "broke" after reaching the pinnacle of success can either drive you to greater success or trap you into a place of immobility. Having a high-level plan that keeps you focused on how you can best leverage your talent and maximize your career potential will at least help you address your fears while still moving forward and having new career experiences.

After more than 40+ years of being afraid of the water, I finally decided I wanted to learn how to swim. I went to my husband who was in the pool for therapy following an auto accident, and I said, "I'm ready." Shortly after, while I was in the pool shivering and deathly afraid, my husband stood in front of me and said, "I'm right here, nothing is going to happen to you. In fact, I want you to think about the worst thing that could happen." After looking at him as if he were crazy, I said I was afraid I would drown. He said, "If that is your worst fear, then try. I want you to put on these goggles, hold your breath, put your head in the water and watch yourself drown." When he challenged me to do the thing I feared the most, I suddenly felt extremely challenged and slightly ticked that he was making fun of me. So I accepted the challenge and quickly sank to the bottom at the four-foot end of the pool. As I sank, I opened my eyes, and because I could see clearly through the goggles, I wasn't as afraid and I let myself float back to the top. I came up out of the water, and I cried, not because I was afraid, but because I had finally attacked a fear. From the point of less fear, I quickly learned how to swim.

> **TWEET WORTHY:**
> "As a football player, I was driven by failure," Strahan says. "I wasn't driven to be successful, per se. Failure meant disappointing my parents, not giving my best, having them look at an effort that they knew was not my best."
> **Michael Strahan**

Fear can have a crippling effect on our lives. Fear of flying keeps us from traveling, fear of heights keeps us from climbing, the fear of rejection keeps us from asking, the fear of commitment keeps us from responsibility, and the fear of failure keeps us from trying. With any one of these fears waving a flag in our lives, who needs enemies and opposition, we are our own worst enemy.

The 7-Step Strategic Brand Plan™ process will challenge you to move beyond the crippling effect of fear to help you create a plan that unlocks a world of possibilities for the unique potential of your brand. You owe it to yourself to maximize every moment, leave nothing on the table, every experience you have – good, bad or indifferent – can be used to your advantage.

How Will A 7-Step Strategic Brand Plan™ Improve My Career Success?

"How did I get here?" Perhaps that is something you've said, or you've heard others say, who find themselves at a place in their careers where they had no intention of being. Because of the technological, medical, and social norms, behaviors and advances that influence the outcome of organizational goals, many organizations have to adopt a six-month checkpoint to assess the progress of their strategic plans and course correct if necessary. The ability to react to new discoveries and discern their usefulness in a timely manner is essential for any organization and any individual who wants to see their ideal future realized. This reaction to change is the primary reason a non-traditional approach to your career is important.

The 7-Step Strategic Brand Plan™ will take you from "How did I get here?" to "What do I do next with what I know?" Just as maps keep you focused and help you navigate rough territory and unexpected detours along a journey, your strategic brand plan will ensure your career goals are organizationally aligned at a high-level. A strategic brand plans keeps you focused, so you can deliver on the emotional promise of the professional experience people have as a result of interacting with you. It is your "how-to" guide to get people to see you the way you want to be seen so you get to do the things you want to do. It is not enough to have talent alone. Your future success requires you to create a strategic approach to see your career goals realized.

> **TWEET WORTHY:**
> "Disruptors don't have to discover something new; they just have to discover a practical use for new discoveries."
>
> **Jay Smith, author**

Every element of the 7-Step Strategic Brand Plan™ is progressive and requires you to identify actions you'll take to move from one element to the next at least every 90 days or sooner.

Explore the Key Elements of Your 7-Step Strategic Brand Plan™

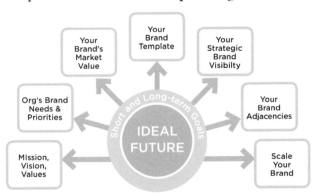

Below is a summary of each element of the plan that will be addressed as you work through this book and build your strategy. Let's delve into the key elements starting with Your Brand Strategy. The other six key elements are summarized here so you can begin thinking about them. Each key element will be discussed in greater detail as you progress in building your brand strategy.

#1 Begin Your Brand Strategy, Write Your Mission

What drives you? Have you ever asked yourself that question? I know I have. Just as Michael Strahan was driven by the idea of failing, I am driven in much the same way. To know what drives you requires that you define what success is for your life, to know your mission in life. Having a mission is like having a Loadstar, a guide, which keeps you focused and motivated. Your mission will be a brief statement of what you want

to do now and how you will do it to move toward your career aspiration. In our 7-Step process, your mission is your career fuel, it encompasses the things you love doing and will help you build a scalable brand. What drives you? What's your purpose? What do you need to learn to achieve your career aspirations?

A. Determine Your Career Aspiration and Non-negotiable Conditions

Why do you exist? Who are you trying to help or serve? What are you looking to achieve? What is/is not acceptable in your work environment, relationships and terms of employment? The answer to these questions can lead you to your career aspiration, or vision, and the ambitious idea of your ultimate goal. By focusing on what you can do to serve others, while also acknowledging those situations that are least motivating, you get a greater sense of how to scale your talent and direct your focus.

Example: My career aspiration is to use music and art to help special needs children excel in their development.

This type of career aspiration will require research, personal and professional development and resource acquisition to be realized over time. For this person, the goal is ambitious because it is what she ultimately sees herself doing, but acknowledges alignment with her organization for talent development as an important step to seeing her ideal future realized. Her non-negotiables, not directly expressed here could include: safe and accessible work environment; to work only with referrals, and/or to not settle on circumstances that involve poor parental support.

B. Write Your Mission

Your personal mission provides clarity about your direction and gives your life a sense of purpose. NASA, for example, states the purpose of space missions is to "…discover new worlds, push the boundaries of our scientific and technical limits…and to address fundamental questions about our place in the Universe and the history of our solar system…"

Likewise, your mission is a summary of what you will do to move toward your career aspiration. And your mission may need to evolve over time in order to remain relevant. An openness to change is necessary and will allow you to adjust to various economic, social, and technological impacts you may encounter. An example of a mission that builds off of the career aspiration above:

Example: To be known by the local special needs community as someone who uses art and music as a way to assist their special needs children excel beyond expectations. I will do this by strengthening my core knowledge of special needs children and families, increase my work with special needs families and communicate successful outcomes.

C. Chart Your Short-term and Long-term Goals

A goal is an observable and measurable outcome that drives you towards a larger plan. If my career aspiration is to "use music and arts to help special needs children…" then my goals need to support this larger more ambitious plan and could include training, development, certifications, etc.

Once you have determined your ideal future, the 7-Step Strategic Brand PlanTM asks you to write down at least three goals that will move you toward the achievement of your ideal future over the next few months to few years.

#2 Identify Your Organization's Brand, Needs and Priorities

What does my organization's brand have to do with my brand? It is a logical question to ask. If your company's brand is about making healthy tasty treats, and you are developing a personal brand centered on music and art therapy, there could be a mission disconnect. There is value in identifying and understanding your organization's role and looking for a connection with your personal goals. At the core, the one thing you both will have in common is the desire for financial success if nothing else. In this step, you'll explore both why and how to identify and align your organization's brand, needs and priorities with your own.

#3 Conduct Your Brand Research

Will there be more or less demand for your talent in the coming years? How will that demand affect your earning potential? These are important questions to explore. It requires you to take a strategic and in-depth look at your future and whether your talent is relevant, marketable and even transferable. In this step, you'll determine the future skills needed for what you want to do and research the industry and businesses in the industry that have success in your ideal future.

#4 Create Your Brand Template

If your brand were a can on a shelf, would it be dented, disheveled and would the package be torn? Or would the presentation of your brand stand head and shoulders above all others? Your Brand Template is how you package and present your talent on a daily basis. If you ignore, reject or skip this step, then you have volunteered to live the life you have instead of the life you want. Dr. Phil famously states "There are no victims, only volunteers." You alone are responsible for how your brand is viewed. The more favorable presentation, the greater the likelihood you'll get to do the things you desire most.

#5 Growing Strategic Brand Visibility

In a room or a business meeting, would you describe your brand as a church mouse or a brave eagle? Which one gets noticed and perhaps taken more seriously? Consider this as you contemplate how you will strategically grow the visibility of your brand. Your leaders must be able to see and experience the best of what you have to offer. Exposure and visibility can build credibility and confidence in your brand, opening doors to new opportunities and experiences, and in this step, I'll show you how to become noticed.

#6 Identify Your Brand Adjacencies™

What if you don't want to do what you're doing for the next ten years? Have you ever considered that you might want to do something different? This step is perhaps the most innovative and powerful in this unique process. I'll help you discover the immense possibilities that await someone with your talent. You can extend your brand in exciting ways while also leveraging your talent for adjacent career opportunities. The most successful and sustainable brands do this best and so can you, I'll show you how.

#7 Scale Your Brand

EVERY brand needs to remain relevant to remain sustainable. In order to be sustainable, your brand needs to be scalable. Your ability to deliver consistent performance at a high level is what leads to brand sustainability. Assess who will help you be accountable for the achievement of your goals and the continued sustainability of your brand.

Take The Journey Of No Risk, No Rewards, No Regrets

Have you heard it said, "When you buy other people's opinion you buy their lifestyle?" This *Think Like A Brand* journey is not for the faint of heart. If you want a breakout career, you'll have to adopt breakout behavior. Stop waiting for something to happen and take the risk required to make it happen.

You choose. You decide whether to trod a traditional path to success: go to school, get a job, wait for a promotion, ask for more money, wait some more, and then wait to retire. Or whether to blaze a new trail that is unique to you, where no path, and only a blueprint, currently exists.

What if I fail? This journey will require you to take some risks, and with risk there is always the possibility of failure. But as Jan C. Ting said, even the *"Illegal immigrants make a rational choice when they decide to violate our immigration laws. They weigh the costs, including the risks of getting caught, against the benefits of a better life."* If you feel you failed at any step in this journey, the good news is you don't get deported or thrown in jail, instead, you get to course adjust and change your path.

In every job I've ever had, I've either been promoted, asked to stay or asked to return, all because of multiple course adjustments. Organizations and leaders change. Therefore, you and I MUST change with them or get lost in the dust. What causes me to make a course adjustment, may cause someone else to wallow in failure. If speaking, writing and being an entrepreneur don't work out for me, guess what, I haven't failed when I move to something new - I've just made a course adjustment!

When Danica McKellar, ended her six-year role as "Winnie Cooper" on the hit TV series "The Wonder Years", she *"was hungry to find out who I was outside of this character everyone loved so much."* Danica's desire to know what else she was capable of outweighed her fear that she'd be *"forgotten completely by the media."*

So she went against traditional wisdom that says, keep working the heck out of Hollywood, and instead she *"went to college and pursued a passion that had nothing to do with acting: mathematics. By the end of an intense four years at UCLA, I had co-authored a new math proof (the "Chayes-*

McKellar-Winn" Theorem), which the media, in fact, loved. As it turned out, math itself blazed my entry back into the spotlight and consequently into wonderful acting jobs like The West Wing and others. You just never know, do you?" By facing her fears, taking risks and learning that she had other talents besides acting, she eventually saw her career come full circle where her love for math and acting are colliding. Not only is she is a three-time New York Times bestselling author, but she is also an internationally-recognized mathematician!

When you move beyond your fear and take the risks necessary to break free from routine, you will start living your life's plan to see your career brand realized. And like Danica, there may be nothing traditional about it. Research is a significant step in your strategic plan. Your research will prepare you for the road less traveled and how to mitigate potential negative circumstances.

Will you accept the *Think Like A Brand* challenge?

√ It's not about me but about who I can serve with my talent. When I consider others, I know the payback is huge!

√ No matter what I do, there is the possibility I will run into people who just won't like me. If this happens, I will determine the importance of the relationship and adjust my plan accordingly.

√ I won't discount entrepreneurship – it works for others, so there is a chance it will work for me.

√ I know that some people will change the rules just because I enter the game. If this happens, I will raise the bar and take my strategy to a whole new level.

√ I will determine if I am in a race of endurance or a fight for freedom. I prefer to endure and stay focused on my goal, rather than to fight and focus on my opponent.

√ I will guard my reputation. It is the key to my credibility, and it is my greatest asset.

√ If I make an exit, I will do so gracefully, keeping my reputation intact.

√ I will seek and accept feedback. I know that successful people are better at handling feedback, and I choose success.

√ When leaders see the subtle improvements or shifts in my conduct, attitude and behavior, I know they may not be prepared or willing to make the shift to meet my

> **TWEET WORTHY:**
> "Fundamental preparation is always effective. Work on those parts of your game that are fundamentally weak."
>
> **Kareem Abdul-Jabbar, retired basketball player**

career needs. If this happens, I won't take it personally. Instead I'll adjust my plan accordingly and keep moving forward.

√   I am in control of my career, not my employer.

√   I will learn to motivate myself.

√   I will live in a constant state of self-development. There is a lot I don't know now that I will need to know later.

√   I will get to know myself and become a student of my audience. Together we will win wars!

Establish A Scalable Brand With This Key Approach

I was watching a season of "The Voice" on NBC and wondered what happened to a few of my favorite vocalists. Thinking to myself, I wondered, "How have they maximized the brand-defining opportunity of being on 'The Voice'?" After searching for a few contestants, I found that many didn't have websites and were lacking in their social footprint. There was relatively little additional newsworthy information available on these individuals who had made such a quick, yet indelible impact on so many viewers. In some ways, this diminishing visibility made sense as I reflected on the repeated lament of "I'm not sure what I'll do" at the thought of being voted off the show. Other comments such as "I'll just go back to working the farm" or "I'll go back to finish school" clarified the lack of brand visibility and helped me understand why they may have faded so quickly from the spotlight.

Might this be a shining example of how many of us are not prepared to fully leverage an opportunity afforded us in our careers? Are we leaving the entirety of our careers in the hands of our voting audience (supervisors, peers, customers)? The good news is, with your motivation, you can effectively use the tools in this book to take the guessing game out of your success, but first you must get prepared!

Save For Your Success

How much does it cost to build a brand? Due to poor financial planning and management, Abraham Lincoln, Walt Disney, Michael Jackson, and even Donald Trump each experienced severe economic woes in the midst of experiencing success. These examples also show you that financial challenges don't have to stop success, but poor planning can significantly slow you down.

> TWEET WORTHY:
> "A wise person should have money in their head, but not in their heart."
>
> **Jonathan Swift, essayist and poet**

The Association for Talent Development's (ATD) *2014 State of the Industry* report states that organizations are spending on average just $1208 per employee for training and development, and this is just 1% more than prior year's spending. On average the number increases by about $600 per employee for smaller organizations and decreases approximately $400 per employee in larger organizations. What's the message? Organizations simply aren't investing in the careers of their employees like they used to. This shift in the allocation of resources by the organization requires the employee to shift how they manage and finance their careers goals.

According to *Building Wealth: A Beginner's Guide to Securing Your Financial Future*, a product of the Federal Reserve Bank of Dallas, the five things we must do to secure our financial future include:

- **Set financial goals**
  How much money will it take to realize your ideal future? How much money would you like to make, realistically on an annual basis? How much can a person with your current skill set make in the next 3-5 years? What will it take to increase your financial income? Will you need additional education and training, and if so, how will these undertakings be financed? If you take out a loan for school, how will you repay it? Establish sound financial goals and hold yourself accountable for achieving them.

- **Budget**
  Do you have a functional budget? A budget is a plan to allocate your future income and manage future expenses. A sound budget is one where you plan to retain more of your income at increasing rates over time than what you spend. According to Investopedia writer, Amy Fontinelle, there are five things a good budget will help you do: 1) help you plan for short and long-term expenses – everything from bills to home-buying, 2) prepare for significant unexpected expenses – such as major medical expenses, 3) keep track of your spending habits so that you'll know where efficiencies can be made, 4) plan for major unexpected life events – such as sudden loss of income or death, and 5) prepare for retirement years.

- **Save and invest**
  How big is your savings account?

> "I wanted to project myself forward to age 80 and say, 'OK, I'm looking back on my life. I want to minimize the number of regrets I have.' And I knew that when I was 80, I was not going to regret having tried this. I was not going to regret trying to participate in this thing called the Internet that I thought was going to be a really big deal. I knew that if I failed, I wouldn't regret that. But I knew the one thing I might regret is not ever having tried. I knew that that would haunt me every day."
>
> **Jeff Bezos**

Saving and investing can put you on the positive side of success following the blueprint of those who have achieved their ideal future by using the money they've earned to finance their goals. LeBron James and Kristi Yamaguchi are excellent examples of how it is done effectively. Both used their athletic and related earnings to finance their future successes because they didn't want to be athletes that ended up bankrupt by the tie their careers ended.

- **Build credit and manage debt**
  What is your credit rating? The better your credit rating, the less risky of an investment you appear to lenders. Debt is not a bad thing, excessive and unmanageable debt is. If you're maxed out now on your credit cards with a lifelong plan to repay the debt, you could find it changes your focus. You begin to focus on doing things to make more money immediately, instead of focusing on a planned path to success. If your credit rating is undesirable, and you have an excessive amount of debt, then establish a plan to pay down or pay off your debt while also improving your credit score. Speak with a financial planning and debt counselor as you plan your ideal future.

- **Protect wealth with basic insurance**
  Did you know insurance is key to wealth building and protection? Insurance plans protect your wealth by guaranteeing payment for injuries or damages to your health and your property. With little to no insurance, you are forced to pay these bills with personal income and savings well into the future. Not paying these bills creates a negative impact on your credit report that could also impact your plans and goals. Consider your family medical history and your own medical history, including recreational activities, when assessing if you are covered adequately. Additionally, property and valuables need coverage, even if renting, to guard against dipping into financial assets in the event of accidents or disasters.

Above all, if you start out testing the waters of your brand as a side-hustle, pay the IRS. Even your side-hustle needs to be accounted for in your financial planning process, your written plans, and your annual tax obligation. Finally, having money and lots of it, doesn't give you a pass on this step. Having money is no guarantee that you know how to manage it. To *Think Like A Brand* is to have a great plan for your success. To *Act Like A Brand* is to practice smart management of your personal and financial resources.

Identify and Embrace Brand-Defining Moments

Would you recognize a big break if it hit you in the head? Being a contestant on a nationally broadcast television program is an excellent public example of a positive brand-defining moment. However, not all brand-defining moments are as easy to detect. An early brand-defining moment for me as a speaker occurred when I spoke for a group on content that I had written. Not only was I new to the job, new as a public speaker, but also new to creating workshop presentations – YIKES! Thank goodness it was a small forgiving crowd. I could feel myself sinking into the floor during the presentation, but since I'm not a quitter, I figured I should at least finish the crappy job I'd started. I can recall the people, their faces, the location, the lighting in the room, the setup and even where I was standing. I can see it as if it just happened yesterday, and although I can laugh now, I was not laughing then. That was a brand-defining moment for me - the point at which I had a negative career experience but used it as motivation to improve, and improve I did! I realized not only how important speaking was to my success on the job, but also to my budding reputation and my career brand. Improving this skill could lead to another marketable talent in my toolkit!

> A Brand-Defining Moment occurs when a positive or negative career experience meets an opportunity to make a change that can either advance or impede your career success.

Judi Sheppard Missett was a professional dancer who decided to extend her brand by teaching dance lessons. It wasn't until her brand-defining moment occurred – attendance steadily declining for her dance classes – that she gained a deeper understanding of what her audience needed; and it wasn't lessons, it was weight loss. Instead of giving up, she used this negative experience to give birth to Jazzercise, a weight loss jazz dance class and a brilliant example of how to take a negative brand-defining moment and turn it into a positive life-changing venture.

As you see, there are positive and negative brand-defining moments, some of the more positive brand-defining moments include:

- Promotions.
- Special assignment to a cool project that allows you to build a new skill or strengthen an existing one.
- Invitation to join a prominent organization.
- Getting hired.
- Providing a solution to a business challenge.

Still many times these defining moments become declining moments when we allow them to slip through our hands:

- Getting fired.
- Being overlooked for a promotion.
- Being marginalized at work.
- A reprimand or write-up.
- Rejection...of any kind.

> "Ask any successful person to look back over the events of his or her life, and chances are there'll be a turning point of one kind or another. It doesn't matter if that success has come on a ball field or in a boardroom, in a research laboratory or on a campaign trail - it can usually be traced to some pivotal moment."
>
> **Bill Rancic**

- Failure at completing a task or assignment.

Often we embrace the good and throw away the bad experiences in life. When really both, working together, thru solid reflection can help us grow and develop in ways that enable us to achieve our goals. Not all defining moments need to be experienced by you, even those experienced by others can shape your thinking and push you into new dimensions. Do you really need to get fired to know the potential impact on your life and your career if unprepared? In fact, just observing a situation, positive or negative, can serve as a powerful defining moment.

Brand-defining moments are those "big breaks" we dream of, and they have the power to motivate us to live our dreams or break us into a million pieces. These experiences are the stuff superstars, entrepreneurs, and highly successful people are made of. Just like a vocalist with a once in a lifetime shot in a vocal competition, the moment can come and go in just the blink of the eye with someone left wondering what happened? Recognize and embrace those impactful career experiences, whether good or bad, and use them for your growth and development.

Change Your Destiny with These Three Words

Can you really prepare for brand-defining moments when you don't know when they will happen? HECK YES! Preparing involves career planning and strategizing. When we plan for success, we can take swifter action to take advantage of opportunities. Take time to think through your response to these three words at your brand-defining moment, if you fail to do so, you will miss out on one more opportunity to fully leverage your brand in a meaningful way:

What happens next?
Just as on shows such as "The Voice", where every single contestant has to face decisions following the end of the show or the day they are voted off, we too must challenge ourselves to consider, **what happens next?** These three little words have the power to help you take four minutes and turn them into a lifetime of living a dream, enjoying a passion and getting paid for it. These three words pack a powerful punch and can help anyone shift from marginalized to maximized in a very short period of time.

The question is not to be asked of others, but of yourself. It is best to ask the question when opportunity knocks, not

> "I remember sitting outside one day, thinking we were three months behind on our house payment, I had two employees I couldn't pay, and I ought to get a real job. But then I thought, No, this is your dream. Recommit and get to work."
>
> **Jill Blashack Strahan,**
> **founder and owner,**
> **Tastefully Simple**

when it has passed. For example, ask "What happens next?" while you're interviewing for an opportunity, or while you're finishing your degree or training program. This is the "thinking" part of the *Think Like A Brand Plan™*. If you don't like your answer, then challenge yourself to change the outcome. If going back to the ranch is not appealing, then what are *you* willing to do to change it?

The feeling that a dream has ended or a moment has passed you by is a terrible feeling and is one of the most critical blows to brand building. The traditional life cycle of every brand is:

- Introduction
- Growth
- Maturity
- Decline

We do well in the introduction and growth stages of our careers. During these phases, we are training, learning, acquiring and strengthening new skills and abilities. But we forget that there is a maturity and decline stage in every career, thus:

- What if I get bored with what I am doing?
- What if my skills are no longer needed?
- What if I outgrow my job?
- What if I'm fired or downsized?

Somewhere between growth and maturity we engage in many defining moments, and those who survive the decline stage do so because they have prepared their brand for these opportunities. In fact they have identified a way to expand their brand in ways that can revive and extend their life cycle through innovation and growth:

- Introduction
- Growth
- Maturity
- Decline
- Innovation
- Growth

Innovation is the introduction of something new or different and is tantamount to the engagement of your defining moment. Your preparation will help you shift quickly from decline to innovation and then growth without missing a beat. The key is to consistently seek to innovate your brand, keep it relevant and alive. Practice the principles found in this book and you'll have a career that is credible, relevant, memorable, likable and extendable.

The difference between being stuck in the Decline Stage and moving into the Innovation and Growth stages depends on how you answer the question, "What

Happens Next?" Consider "what happens next" or variations of this question with every career turning point, good or bad. Projecting ahead of each career phase and considering alternative endings is the only way to keep your brand alive. Let's look at this again:

- What if I get bored or am unsatisfied with what I am doing? *What can I do next?*
- What if my skills are no longer needed? *What alternatives do my talents afford me?*
- What if I outgrow my job? *Where can my talents take me?*
- What if I'm fired or downsized? *What can I make happen next?*

> TWEET THIS:
> **"You can ensure your brand-defining moment does not become a brand-declining moment - #strategizing, #planning, and #action." #careers #TLAB**

Every brand reading this book will go through the first four stages of the life cycle at varying rates. You can ensure your brand-defining moment does not become a brand-declining moment through strategizing, planning, and action. The next two steps will better prepare you to recognize your brand-defining moments, to leverage and to maneuver them.

Chapter Summary

How do you "Michael Strahan" your brand?

1. Start thinking now about your future. Michael didn't wait until football ended to begin strategizing about his next career move, and neither should you.
2. Be bold and willing to try new things in areas where your brand and character can carry you, even things that break with tradition and stretch your comfort zone.
3. Research the success of others with similar brands. What can you learn from their experiences to add value to your own?
4. Build your strategy by determining what drives you. Michael was driven by fear of failure, from there he became unstoppable. What about you?
5. Adopt breakout behavior and look for ways to make things happen for your brand.
6. Accept the *Think Like A Brand* Challenge.
7. Save for your success. Organizations are not investing as much as they used to in their employees. What will you do with the investment they make in training and development dollars for you and with the salary you earn?
8. Identify and embrace brand-defining moments; moments that occur when a positive or negative career experience meets with an opportunity for you to make a

change that can either advance or impede your career success.

9. Learn to repeatedly ask and act on the question, "What happens next?"

Waiting for someone to offer you an opportunity is the old way of managing your brand. The "Michael Strahan" blueprint calls for proactively preparing for and going after what you want!

IDENTIFY YOUR ORGANIZATION'S BRAND, NEEDS AND PRIORITIES

> "I am not an oligarch. I am a servant and I try to align my interests and those of my investors."
>
> *Yuri Milner, Entrepreneur*

Jeff Bezos

Business magnate, investor, and technology entrepreneur

Jeff Bezos knows how to identify an organization's brand, needs and priorities. He is the well-known founder and CEO of Amazon.com - one of the largest retailers on the internet, and he used his education and work experiences to build intellectual capital through some very strategic career moves.

He began nurturing the entrepreneurial bug by launching his first business in high school - The DREAM Institute - an educational summer camp for grade school youth. Jeff's career took off after graduating from Princeton and working in computer sciences on Wall Street. From there he scaled his brand to work in a number of for-profit and publically traded organizations including Bankers Trust and the investment firm D.E. Shaw & Company.

While his brand in finance was highly profitable, he used his profitability and his track record for identifying an organization's brand, needs and priorities to move into the promising world of e-commerce, moving to Seattle and opening an online bookstore. Now with Amazon as a top model for Internet sales, Bezos has turned his attention toward other ventures including the purchase of "The Washington Post" newspaper. This business leader truly embodies our second *Think Like A Brand* Secret:

SECRET #2:
Lean in to the future because complaining isn't a strategy.

"What we need to do is always lean in to the future; when the world changes around you and when it changes against you - what used to be a tail wind is now a head wind - you have to lean into that and figure out what to do because complaining isn't a strategy."

Jeff Bezos

Accept and Lean In To Reality

If I stop complaining, will my voice be heard? Surprise, complainers get cut from the team, not elevated because of their complaint. In reality, there are some organizations that need lots of culture work behind the scenes despite their public success, but there are no perfect organizations.

I recall giving a keynote speech and speaking about why there will never be a perfect organization and one lady shouted out, "Because where there are people, there are problems!" We all laughed but darned if she weren't telling the truth.

According to noted psychologist and emotional intelligence expert, Daniel Goleman, if you are going to elevate the image of your brand you need to have a healthy balance of three things:

1. Inner focus. A focus on your needs, goals and priorities.
2. Other focus. A desire to help others be successful including peers, teammates and leaders.
3. Outer focus. An eye towards the systems around us that help us navigate our lives, organizations and world structures.

Notice that two of the three are a focus on someone and something other than yourself? Build your brand while focusing on the needs of others, for as the organization is being elevated, so are you:

"The rising tide lifts all the boats."

John F. Kennedy

Keep in mind, however, that shameless self-promotion, inconsistent performance, and unprofessional behavior can all damage a personal brand. Fortunately, poor branding can be mitigated with brand alignment, trusted mentors and coaches, and a reliable system of feedback and on-going development.

Identify and Align to Improve a Suffering Brand Image

Why do I need to identify and align my goals with the organization's? This is a common question I get when coaching around performance improvement and career strategy.

There are a couple of important reasons:

- Your organization is the primary investor of your brand; Charlie Sheen forgot this for a moment.
- You are getting paid to play: test new ideas, concepts, strategies, and methodologies that have the potential for positive impact and outcomes. These experiences become part of your intellectual capital and your brand experience record.
- Your motivation gets a boost, and you get to acquire new skill sets.
- As the organization's brand is elevated, so is yours. You get to be part of their success and reputation.
- Your financial growth is tied directly to the financial growth of the organization.

According to a report by the global management consulting firm, Bain & Company, only 40% of the workforce of organization's surveyed knew about the company's goals, strategies, and tactics. Competing priorities result in fragmented and lackluster outcomes. No organization wants to compete with the employee's priorities and neither should it have to. If you find out, in your research of the organization's brand, needs and priorities that there is nothing you can align with, then look for an organization where you can. You'll be a much happier employee in the long run.

When you link your personal brand to that of the organization's brand, needs, and priorities, you'll find that a shared understanding of purpose creates consistency in performance, in the employee and in the organization. Let's examine at least five ways to make this happen.

Step One: Study the Organization

Learn everything about the company you currently work for in a manner that makes it easy for you to know how and when you can showcase your brand. Successful entertainment brands learn everything they can about their industries. This knowledge gives them ideas about options that may be available to them down the line. Employees who consider the big picture are better able to see all the different ways their talent can be useful.

TWEET WORTHY:
"The more extensive a man's knowledge of what has been done, the greater will be his power of knowing what to do."

Benjamin Disraeli, former British Prime Minister

One evening my son had the television tuned to the Disney Channel and during a Disney moment, they discussed how two of the Channel's young actors voiced interest in learning how to direct episodes. As a result, they were coached and later given opportunities to direct a few of them. Even our younger professionals are learning how important it is to diversify and extend the life of their brands.

Likewise, with so many employees to manage, it is difficult for managers to single out employees and fully consider all they might have to offer. Therefore, it is incumbent upon each employee to take responsibility for their own success by providing the leader with enough information about their talent that it becomes easy for the leader to tap them for opportunities.

I was sitting in the next room listening to my 13-year-old participate in his first job interview. During the interview, he was asked, "Why do you want this job?" He paused for a moment and responded, "Because one day I want to run my own business, and I figure I should learn how to work for someone else first." "Wow", I thought to myself, he gets it. He understands that being an entrepreneur looks cool from the outside, but he knows from living with me and his dad that there is a lot of work and lot to be learned about being an employee – let alone running a business of your own.

There is so much to learn from your company. Join the 40% of employees in the workforce, reported by Bain and Company, who know about their company's goals, strategies and tactics. They are leveraging their knowledge in ways that boosts their careers and the organization's goals.

> **TWEET THIS:**
> "Learn everything about your employer in a manner that makes it easy 4u2 know how and when you can showcase your #brand." #careers #TLAB

Finally, take the time to learn how your organization makes money, loses money, and approaches customers. This information and insight will help you truly understand all the mechanics of running a business and help you identify opportunities for deeper engagement and brand development.

Step Two: Get Your Head in the Game - Align with the Company
Try thinking from the point of view of the owner, CEO or executive. Use what you learned in Step Two to inform your thinking. Approach your work and personal interactions being "other focused". From this point of view you will begin to see not only how your talents might be utilized, but also how the talents of others might be further employed in the organization.

What do I do with this information? Ever see a person in a meeting whom you know is knowledgeable, and has great ideas, just sit there without offering input? Ever try to prompt them to speak up and see the look of either apathy or fear in their eyes? Don't let this be you, and if it is you, push past the fear, push past the apathy and make your voice heard. Think of it as practice for something bigger.

I hate being forced to think critically on the spot. I am one of those people who prefers to get information in advance, read, digest and meditate, so I can be prepared before walking into meetings. So when I'm forced out of this comfort zone, and this happens often, I turn to my coaching training and experience and ask powerful thought-provoking questions. This accomplishes several things. In addition to pulling me out of my comfort zone, it has a way of deepening the discussion and also promoting a higher level of thinking in the room. Here's what else you can do:

- Look for solutions to problems.
- Use what you know to forecast challenges.
- Offer viable solutions.
- Keep the customer in mind – what do you know about them?
- Who else needs to be included in the discussion? Are they in the room?
- Tap the quiet contributors; sometimes they need a gentle nudge to speak up.
- Focus on the outcomes - what are we really trying to accomplish?

This can be challenging, but you'll find that your thinking is supported by your behavior and vice versa.

Once you are exposed to a new way of scaling your brand, you won't go back to career management as usual – waiting for someone to tap you on the shoulder, waiting to be noticed, waiting for that promotion or special assignment. Instead, you'll open the door to new possibilities just by developing an "outer focus" and an "other focus".

> **TWEET WORTHY:**
> "A mind that is stretched by a new experience can never go back to its old dimensions."
>
> **Oliver Wendell Holmes, Jr., Former Associate Justice of the Supreme Court of the United States**

Step Three: Master Your Current Job

Are you the master of your brand? Your job is within your control. Upon hire or promotion, you were awarded ownership to a thing called "your job" and as such, an investment is being made in you regardless of whether you want the job long-term or not. Even if there are people who pose as leaders trying to marginalize and undermine your success, you still are in control.

I recall being pinned under the hand of a succession of really bad bosses. For a slight second I thought God needed a good laugh choosing me for the gig. They worked hard to make my life a living hell. Saying "no" to strategies I'd propose, adopting my proposals as their own – the ones they liked anyway, looking for ways to reprimand my every move, and marginalizing me to such a degree that I could no longer recognize my original job. What a fresh hell this was. The sad thing is, I loved my job, hid most of my pain from the outside world, and continued to perform the best I could. I focused on the organization's brand, its needs and priorities and took lemon after lemon and made a fresh batch of lemonade – whoa, did that piss them off and their little friends too! Still I hung on, stayed engaged and kept drinking in everything I could about the organization because I

knew, someday, I would not be there, and I would not be robbed of the opportunity to use this experience to my advantage. In fact, one person said to me at the onset of the promotion a few years prior, "Pam, your job is to learn everything you can about this job, it won't last forever," and that is exactly what I did. Fast forward, that experience and the knowledge I gained from understanding that organization's brand, needs, and priorities, is what helped me think about how I strategize and run my business today.

Having brand control and finding success is not easy in trying circumstances. Just as building muscle mass increases your metabolic rate, your ability to burn more fat and have more energy - when you successfully hurdle challenging work situations by effectively completing the task and achieving the goal despite the roadblocks, you decrease the impact future challenges will have on your brand. You build brand muscle every time you successfully hurdle a tough situation. Soon, people will come to you for advice, insights and coaching for their own brand management.

Step Four: Reinvest Their Investment

What did you do with your investment dollars? As I've stated before, look at your salary, bonus and benefits as a type of investment the organization is making in your brand. Every time you score a win in a job well-done, they receive a return on that investment and you are rewarded with a continued deposit of investment dollars in the form of a paycheck.

If the organization is not investing in the maintenance of your brand through training and development, then that responsibility belongs to you. Set aside a percent of your salary every pay towards brand development. Next, because of the speed of organizational change, you never know if a reorganization will suddenly impact the continued flow of investment dollars. Set aside an additional amount to help support you financially should you need to search for another home for your brand.

Doing these three things will help you feel more secure and give you a sense of peace about sudden disruptions to the flow of investment dollars currently pouring in.

Step Five: Be More Than a Team Player

Why is being a team player and being responsible not enough? Because organizations feel that is what they pay you for, it is expected of you from day one. While these talents are relevant to any job, organizations are looking for your brand to offer more. For example, instead of just being a team player, are you able to step out and become a team leader? Instead of just being responsible, can you be responsible and resourceful?

Here's what I want you to get from this chapter, if you have a job, why not use it to your advantage. Learn everything you can about the organization and become a student of your company. There is so much to be gained in intellectual capital that once you get started you'll find that aligning your goals with the company's is easier than initially thought. Run with it.

Chapter Summary

How do you "Jeff Bezos" your brand?

1. Learn as much as you can about doing business through formal education experiences and through careful research about your employer's brand, needs and priorities.
2. Figure out how to align your brand with your employer's – they are an investor in your brand. The more they experience a return on their investment, the greater the potential investment in your brand grows.
3. Use the return on those investment dollars to reinvest in building and developing your talent and creating career options.
4. Boost intellectual capital by understanding how the organization operates; how they make money, lose money and the behavior of their customers. This information will be useful as you strengthen your talent portfolio.
5. Master your job. It might not be the thing you want to do in the long run but don't waste it away by complaining. Instead, focus on how you can use what you do to transition into something else.
6. Become a resourceful leader. Pull from your knowledge base and use your talent to lead initiatives and explore new ways of helping the organization - and you - find success.

Jeff Bezos continues to build the value of his brand because he understands the needs of his customer. Right now, your primary customer is your employer. Seek to understand their needs and priorities, making them your own, and you too will experience the type of success you desire.

RESEARCH THE FUTURE DEMAND FOR YOUR TALENT

"As an entrepreneur, one of the biggest challenges you will face will be building your brand.... If you form a strategy without doing the research, your brand will barely float — and at the speed industries move at today, brands sink fast."

Ryan Holmes, Founder and CEO, Hootsuite

Misty Copeland

Ballet dancer, spokesperson, and role model

Misty Copeland is a ballet dancer who, in 2015, amidst a challenging upbringing and against odds, became the first African American female principal dancer with the American Ballet Theatre (ABT). A unique aspect of Misty's career as a ballet dancer is that she did not start ballet at the typical age of 7 to 10. Her first formal encounter with ballet was at age 13 – considered a late start for a serious dance career.

However with an intensive training schedule, at age 15 she won first prize for ballet at the Los Angeles Music Center Spotlight Awards. Shortly thereafter, she received a full scholarship into the San Francisco Ballet. Despite years of custody battles between her mother and her guardians, she returned to live with her family. Studying ballet at Lauridsen Ballet Centre in Torrance, California led to another full scholarship in 2000 to the ABT's intensive summer program. That year she was also named the ABT's National Coca-Cola Scholar. In 2001, Misty became a member of the ABT's corps de ballet and the only African American woman in a group of 80 dancers.

Constantly reminded of differences in her body type and race as compared to most in ballet, she worked tirelessly to ascend to the top in the field. Because of her exceptional talent and hard work, in 2007 Misty became the company's first African American female soloist in more than 20 years.

Misty's inspirational story has made her a role model. In 2009, she appeared in a music video by Prince and also performed live with him on tour in 2010. A strong advocate for the diversification of ballet for dancers of varying racial and financial backgrounds, she has served as a mentor and published her memoir in 2014. For this reason, Misty exemplifies our third *Think Like A Brand* Secret:

"Some people even think that I'm still just not right for it [ballet]. And I think it's shocking because they hear those words from critics saying I'm too bulky, I'm too busty. And then they meet me in person and they're like, you look like a ballerina. And I think it's just something maybe that I will never escape from, those people who are narrow-minded. But my mission, my voice, my story, my message, is not for them. And I think it's more important to think of the people that I am influencing and helping to see a broader picture of what beauty is."

Misty Copeland

Knowing what you want to do and how you want to make your mark is a powerful feeling. It gives you confidence in yourself and empowers you to have a place of influence. If you want to display confidence, then you'll want to know that your brand, your talent, are in demand for the long run. Research can give you the confidence you need to become a person of influence.

Uncover Your Career Shelf Life

Where are you in the brand life cycle? To answer questions about your career shelf life, you'll need to know where you are in the life cycle. Someone like Misty, at her age and level, is headed towards the decline stage in her career and is no doubt exploring innovation and growth opportunities for the next phase of her highly talented and popular brand.

Similar to the career of a professional athlete, statistically a dancer's career can begin to taper off in their 30's. An individual who decides to pursue a dance career, especially in ballet, needs to know this and understand the rigorous effect on the body from years of intense training and development. Likewise, we too need to be aware of the "shelf life" of our careers. Being able to look around the corner to see what the demand will be is fundamental to the sustainability of your brand. In addition, you'll want to know how much time and resources to invest in your brand development if it has a shorter shelf life than other careers where your talent can be leveraged.

The door is open to any number of things for Misty because of her talent, visibility, and popularity.

> **TWEET THIS:**
> **Every #brand every #career has a shelf life. Have you looked around the corner to see yours? #branding #TLAB**

Clearly capable, competent and credible, she is an attractive talent for those looking for someone to represent their brand. She is being tapped by Under Armour, Prince and others to help elevate their brands, while also strengthening her own. However this opportunity is not guaranteed for everyone and does not come easily. Let's learn why research is important and how to go about doing it.

Clarify the Importance of Brand Research

What does research have to do with building a brand? With advances in telephony, automation exchanges, computers and refrigeration - switchboard operators, typesetters, the milkman and, yes, the elevator operator, are among the many jobs that are now extinct. Today, economists and researchers report that due to advances in technology alone, we can expect to see jobs such as call center operators, travel agents, secretaries, cashiers, postal workers, and even bank tellers become extinct in the coming years. Millions of lives will be impacted in the future, including the residual effect of those who interact with these individuals as part of their normal work routines every day.

This is why research is important. It will help you determine the current and future demand for your talent helping you make an informed decision about your career and perhaps even helping your organization prepare for the impact economic, social, political, technological and legal changes will have on organizational goals.

In addition to the occupational outlook for your talent, your research should inform you of different career variations, how much you can expect to make by level and region, qualification requirements, and the organizations typically in search of various talents.

Develop Your Brand Research Questions

What questions will guide my research? You'll want to spend time interviewing people you find successful in your field, reading books, doing an internet search, etc.
to gather information about the extent to which you can grow your brand. Some examples include:

1. What will be the demand for this talent in the next 20 years?
2. What are the trends that could influence demand?
3. What are the local, national, and global job demands?
4. What are the types of career tracks available to someone with my talent?
5. What education, skills, abilities, languages and/or experience are required?

6. What is happening that is creative in this area of talent or career?
7. What is the range in pay? Why does it vary? How can I get the maximum market value for my talent?
8. How will I determine my level of satisfaction in the long run?
9. What do I need to do to be successful?
10. How will I finance my plan for sustainable success?

The answers to these questions will require you to speak with people who are successful in careers today that you seek to achieve tomorrow. You should also spend time at a library and online, researching information for these answers and compare them to the answers you receive when you speak with people personally. Speak not only with people who are active in the area of success you seek, but also those who are part of their audience, people who lead, manage or are otherwise responsible for developing talent. This information will inform your overall 7-Step Strategic Brand PlanTM.

List Your Marketable Talents

What are your talents on the table? These are skills, abilities, and strengths that your employer, and the market, finds valuable and for which you shine at work and enjoy performing. These are the hard skills (the "what" you do well) that make up your areas of excellence, such as the design of computer programs or your certifications in a particular area of work. These talents are so well-developed and marketable that they have the power to allow you to stand alone as an entrepreneur performing this talent if you would so choose.

Back in the early 1980's the U.S. saw a growing increase in the number of people who called themselves professional organizers. These are individuals who realized they had a strength to help others achieve a repeatable system for order. Their system helped individuals and businesses reduce clutter and turn mountains of paper, boxes, and excessive untidiness (to put it nicely) into a personal repeatable system of organization. According to the National Association of Professional Organizers, their organization grew from just a few women in a living room with a marketable talent for putting things in order and to a membership that today boasts over 4,000 members worldwide. The pioneers in this field recognized they had a strength that others found valuable and that the strength had the power to stand on its own as a business. If they were to complete this exercise they might write down their strength as "helping people be more efficient with their time."

We could have simply listed the strength as "help people get organized" but that is a bit trite and doesn't make me want to learn more; it doesn't grab me and pull me in so that I ask the question, "How do you do that?" You want people to be inquisitive about you, so get in the habit of talking about outcomes. What does your talent do for others? What are the benefits they receive as a result of hiring you or working with you? Make the listener want to lean in and learn more. Some other examples include:

Good	Better
Ability to work remotely.	Complete projects and achieve business outcomes by working in a solo environment.
Bilingual: English and Mandarin	Leverage bilingual skills (English and Mandarin) to close foreign business deals and boost customer engagement.
Business Development	Boost long-term business value by more than 10% annually through the development of relationships with new and existing customers, key stakeholders and the analysis of markets.
Statistical Analysis and Data Mining	Improve revenue generation through statistical analysis and data mining.

This is not "spin" which is deceptive language historically used in public relations to persuade the public for or against an issue, topic, event or campaign. "Spin" communication has found its way into the world of "resume spin doctors" who enlarge your talents on paper in an effort to help you attract job opportunities. If you are honest about how your talent has benefited an organization, then you don't need someone to "spin" your resume into a web of deceptive and manipulative lies that you have to maintain.

Instead your goal is to emphasize how another individual or organization has benefited from exposure to your talent. When a recruiter is looking to fill a technical role, or a business leader is seeking a consultant to help them achieve a technical need, they are likely to be very specific about their requirements. Likewise, you will want to be very specific about your technical talent achievements.

Now you are in a position to express your most valuable and marketable talents, verbally and in writing, during interviews, while networking, and in performance reviews and discussions with leaders.

What if I don't know what my talents are?

Many of us have built our careers based on filling a business need. Typically we start our career after high school or college and take just about any job that sounds remotely interesting with a decent salary and voila, a career is unwittingly born. If we never revisit

> "You discover yourself through the research of your work."
>
> **Carine Roitfeld,**
> **editor**

our research on the demand for our talent, we might end up following an employer-designed career that meets the employer's need but never addresses our own.

Before I help you determine your talent, promise me this – that you will be honest with yourself. If you are not, this next step will do you no good, and you'll find yourself revisiting this chapter again in about six to twelve months.

Pull out a piece of paper and draw a line down the center of the paper. At the top on the left side, write the words, "People Come to Me Most Often For...." Here you are going to capture the specific skills and abilities for which you appear to be a go-to-person personally and professionally. A hint: you probably get consistent high marks on your performance review in these areas. These represent your strengths. For example: delivering presentations, content design and development, customer relationship building, team development, collaborate on projects, lead projects, research, rebuild relationships, solve business problems, mediate situations, edit writing, etc.

This exercise is important because we can take our natural gifts for granted, they can be easily overlooked as a talent or even as a strength. When I have highlighted this during coaching sessions, people often look at me strangely and say, "That? Oh it's just something I do!" as if it shouldn't count, but that "something" can mean everything to someone who wants to successfully manage their brand.

I recall taking on a tough interim CEO assignment in an organization that struggled in many areas, one of those being compliance. What was interesting is that my finance director showed phenomenal compliance skills – a business need that was decentralized and unorganized at the time of my interim assignment. He jumped in to help me unravel the compliance puzzle because it was just "easy" for him to do. His competence in the area of compliance seemed natural and something he enjoyed! In fact, I began to quickly leverage his skills as if he were the compliance officer for the organization. He helped us get into compliance with relative ease because I released him to do what he didn't know he loved doing. Now, I'd like to say it was genius on my part to recognize his skills, but really it was his willingness to step up and help me fill a gap, when he really didn't have to. From there, he was able to identify a marketable talent that he could use to build his brand template.

Now, on the right side of that line, write the words, "Things I Love to Do." In this list, you're going to write the type of things you would do if all jobs paid the same. You are looking for a career that pays you a competitive salary that you might really enjoy doing for a long time. If a hobby such as crocheting (I know, a huge stretch but work with me here) is something you would love to get paid to do, then write it down with an open mind. You'll see how this plays out later on, but again, be honest with yourself, and remember there is always room for error; we've built that into the model.

At this point your paper should look like this:

People Come to Me Most Often For	*Things I Love to Do*
• Advice on how to work with a difficult customer. • To lead complex team projects. • Help resolving interpersonal conflict.	• Mentoring and helping people solve problems. • Working with children. • Playing Tennis.

The final step in discovering your talents is to review both columns and find synergy. What do these two columns say about the type of work you should be doing? What jumps out at you? There are always aspects of our work we don't "love" doing, but if we have a skill in an area, we find a way to use the things we do well to fuel the things we love. If we take the above example, this person might not like leading team projects, but her skills in this area could help her find satisfaction in a career that involves leading a project team that involves children. Or leading a project that helps parents overcome challenges with their children.

So what are her talents - her cognitive, technical or interpersonal skills, developed or learned through training and/or experience?

- Converts challenging people experiences into profitable business results.
- Inspires and motivates teams to achieve goals, beat deadlines, and produce revenue.
- Avoids costly mistakes by challenging conventional thinking.
- Bridges cross-generational communication challenges.

> TWEET THIS:
> "Your #talent, not your job's title is what makes you valuable." #careers #branding #TLAB

When you evaluate your work in this way, you can begin to see how your talent, not a job title, is what makes you valuable. Play with this a minute. When you tell an interviewer that your strengths include communicating with people, especially difficult people, and she asks, "How do you know?" You can reply with confidence, "Because I am often sought out for advice on how to work with difficult customers, and also how to address interpersonal conflicts between others. In fact, I enjoy mentoring and helping people solve problems." That interviewer sees more than a candidate for a job and instead sees an individual who gets a spot on her team, and THAT is what we're after. Companies will create jobs for people with talent!

How do I know if my talent is marketable?

Having a strength in a certain area of our skills does not always translate into the marketability of that skill. Need drives marketability. Research is important in this step because it helps you assess the present and future need for your talents:

- Conduct online research.
- Speak with people who are at higher levels in your field.
- Call and speak with your local college and university career services office.
- Contact recruiters and search agencies.
- Research the growth/decline in pay for someone with your talent.
- Check out Occupational Outlook through the Bureau of Labor Statistics.

All of these research methods will help you determine if this is a skill that you should focus on and continue to develop, or if you should focus more on developing an underutilized area of your talent. You might discover that you have a talent that is untapped in the marketplace but for which you see a clear need, just like the early professional organizers who realized they had a talent they believed could stand on its own.

Remember that need drives innovation. Even if you find very little information in your research, consider what you know about this talent of yours that could be innovative as either a stand-alone talent in the market, such as becoming a professional organizer, or that an employer could find highly valuable.

Identify Your Key Competencies

What competencies will keep my career sustainable? Competencies are the observable and measurable conduct, attitude and behaviors that bring emphasis to the knowledge, skills, and abilities that distinguish an individual's performance in the work environment. It is the "how" you do what you do so well. Your ability to define and master competencies will lead you to the type of career success you desire. According to research on the competencies displayed by successful people, a short compilation of the abilities they have in common include being:

- solution oriented
- ambitious, decisive
- focused, resilient
- motivated towards achievement
- doers
- visionary
- resourceful

Many employers and professionals list key competencies required for mastery in a given role in their organization. It is the difference in being known as an IT professional and a "solutions-oriented" IT professional. Which would you prefer to hire? Many associations have competencies they believe critical to your success in a given field of practice. Think about your core competencies and add them to your brand template.

Chapter Summary

How do you "Misty Copeland" your brand?

1. Recognize your mission, your voice, your story and your message are all part of your brand and have a place of influence. Regardless of your socio-economic background and experiences, you can develop a brand that is viewed and received as capable, competent and credible.

2. Assessing where you are in the brand lifecycle will help you determine your brand's shelf life. Misty is a unique brand, with a strong story and mission. She has been given a platform from which to showcase her brand. This alone has the effect of extending the shelf life of her brand. However, even without a public platform, you can extend your brand through innovation and creativity.

3. Conduct thorough research about the demand for your brand 10-20 years from now. Misty will likely not be dancing at the same level. However, she'll need to know if the popularity of this work is one she can leverage into the future. Perhaps even opening her own ballet studio. This research can inform the various career options you have to extend the life of your brand as well.

4. List your marketable talents. The talents that organizations are willing to invest time and resources for and which are your strengths.

5. Determine your key competencies. This is the "how" you do what you do so well and what will lead to a sustainable career.

Misty Copeland is living research. Her life experiences coupled with her talent have provided us with a living observatory of how you build a brand amidst challenge and adversity. All of us will face varying degrees of challenge as we build our brands, we can use Misty's experience as an example of how to stare down adversity and press on to higher heights. Take your research seriously. It is foundational and will inform the next step in Thinking Like A Brand, the development of your brand template.

CREATE YOUR BRAND TEMPLATE

"Multipotentiality is the state of having many exceptional talents, any one or more of which could make for a great career for that person."

Tamara Fisher, education specialist

Taylor Swift

Singer, songwriter, actress, and philanthropist

To say that Taylor Swift is making an impact on a daily basis is an understatement. There are no words to describe how or why she has exploded onto the pop culture scene and has been able to command the type of attention and respect unheard of in quite some time.

At the age of 14 Taylor moved to Nashville, Tennessee to pursue a career in country music. After the release of her self-titled first album in 2006, her country music soared, garnering her a Best New Artist nomination at the 2008 Grammy Awards. Her second album became the bestselling album of 2009, winning four Grammy Awards and she made history as the youngest artist ever to win Album of the Year. Taylor continues to win Grammy Awards, American Country Music Awards, American Music Awards, etc. and is recognized globally, winning prestigious awards in Canada, Thailand, Germany, Australia, and Japan to name a few. She also holds four music related Guinness World Records.

Taylor has packaged her brand in such a way that she is more than a household name in many respects. Instead, "Taylor Swift" is an adjective that means breakout phenomenon. Taylor's ability to show her humanity through her music, her website, her Instagram pics and her twitter comments, allows others to connect with her brand in a seemingly very personal way.

The foundation of Taylor's business empire rests in her ability to consistently package her talent so that she is making a positive impact and impression on the lives of her fans and all those on-lookers who scratch their heads and say to themselves, "Where did she come from?"

Still for all of her accolades, honors, awards, and myriad of "firsts", I give Taylor one additional recognition as the symbol of our fourth *Think Like A Brand* Secret:

SECRET #4:
Hold yourself accountable for excellence. You are the only one who will get to decide what you will be remembered for.

"I hope you know that you've given me the courage to change. I hope you know that who you are is who you choose to be, and that whispers behind your back don't define you. You are the only one who gets to decide what you will be remembered for."

Taylor Swift

Branding is how you market and present yourself. Your brand is the emotional promise of the experience people will have as a result of interacting with you. It is apparent that Taylor Swift is making an indelible impression with her brand both personally and professionally. Her emotional promises keep creating opportunities for her to market and present her talent before an eager audience of fans and spectators.

Taylor's excellence in music is how she has taken ownership for her brand and opened the door to a powerful Brand Template. Your brand template is wrapped in a reputation for excellence in at least one area of your talent. Master it, embrace it, showcase it and leave your audience wanting more in such a way that they are willing to open new doors just for the opportunity to experience more of you.

You know you are delivering excellence in an area of your talent when:

√ You receive high marks for performance.
√ Others speak positively about you when you're not in the room.
√ You're called upon to help with special assignments or tasks that involve someone with your talent or expertise.
√ You are confident about your ability to deliver results.
√ You are relied upon for delivering excellence.
√ You are given responsibilities above and beyond the average performer.
√ You are given opportunities to try new things that might appear outside of your area of expertise.
√ You are sought out for your opinion and advice in work related matters.
√ You are asked to serve outside of the organization due to your reputation and talent excellence.

As you prepare to build or strengthen your Brand Template, consider the degree to which it reinforces what you want people to think about you. Everything you do, everywhere you go, everything you say - you are marketing your brand. What is the message that is being received by others and is it the message you intend to convey? When we take ownership of the management of our brand, we take responsibility for delivering a consistent brand message that is capable, credible, and competent.

Seek to operate from a place of excellence and your talent will make room for you in new and exciting ways.

Assess Your Brand's Impact and Influence

What talents are you bringing to the table? This is the intersection and interplay between what you love, what you want, and what you're good at doing.

Why do I need a Brand Template if I am already delivering excellence?
In an interview with Oprah Winfrey, Dee Snyder of famed rock band Twisted Sister made this statement:

"The biggest thing that surprised me about fame was that it was fleeting, you work so hard to get there and you just assume that it is some kind of finish line. You take a victory lap or maybe spike the ball, you know and maybe run around the field screaming GOAL! I don't know,.....I was not prepared for my career to end as dramatically as it did and the ego that makes you believe that you're gonna succeed won't allow you to believe that it's over. So the big mistake I made and that people make is that you start borrowing against your future you know because the next album will get it, the next band, the next tour and then all of a sudden I had nothing."

During the great recession of 2007-2009, The International Labor Organization estimated that the number of jobless worldwide reached about 212 million in 2009, an increase of 34 million compared with 2007. How many of the 212 million jobless believed they were delivering excellence just the year before they were laid off? Plants close, companies move, and other organizations make significant shifts in direction – all affecting excellent workers who were "not prepared for their careers to end as dramatically as they did."

Thinking Like A Brand requires you to work to establish at least three talents of excellence which, when faced with dramatic changes, could make for great career options and alternatives. Taylor Swift's talents, for example, include singing, songwriting, and acting. If Taylor's music sales were to steadily decline, she could move to focus on a career as a songwriter or move into acting, producing, and other aspects of the music business.

Values Exercise

What will guide my decisions, conduct, attitude and behavior, such that people have a positive professional experience with me? Values are those closely held beliefs and standards of behavior that guide us to what is important in our lives. Our values dictate our behavior, decisions, and attitudes towards just about everything. They are the "why" we do what we do. Knowing your values in a way is knowing what makes you happy, what brings you satisfaction, and from a career standpoint, this is very important.

To determine your core values, answer these questions:

- What have been your three greatest accomplishments?
- If you could change one thing in the world, what would it be and why?
- Identify times in your life when you have been happiest?
- What issues get you the most fired up when you talk about them or hear others talking about them? Why do those issues affect you in this way?
- Identify the times when you were most fulfilled in your career?
- Think of another moment in your life that was really satisfying or fulfilling for you. What was that moment and what made you feel that way about it?

What themes emerge about your values? If there are key words that are common in your answers, write them down and create a list of your core values. Some examples include:

Faith	*Ambition*	*Thoroughness*	*Integrity*	*Respect*
Family	*Excellence*	*Consistency*	*Health*	*Love*
Fun	*Achievement*	*Creativity*	*Adventure*	*Support*

This list is not exhaustive, there are hundreds of words that describe values. Identify your top five and build them into your Talent Template. In order for you to experience maximum career satisfaction, you should consider your values in every career decision you make.

Evaluate Your Brand's Career Progression

How do I know if I am making progress? Have you ever imposed an imaginary measuring stick when looking at your career, and does it often involve comparing your career with someone else's? Bad move. Even if you share the same job and life experiences as another, you're still different. Your values, competencies, and even the details of your life experiences contribute to what makes you unique.

To be fair, we still like a way of determining if we are making progress. Below is a progress chart that will help you examine the degree to which you might be progressing through your career.

First let's begin with an evaluation of your brand's career progression. The three outer circles, average to solid performer, are trademarks of a typical career. The goal of *Think Like A Brand* is to move you into high potential and top talent status where your brand is positioned for innovation and growth, equating to a brand that is viewed as capable, credible, and competent with extendable opportunities.

Average Performer. This is the introduction stage of your brand. The place where you are showcasing your talent and even strengthening existing skillsets. Decision-makers observe your talent and contributions.

Emerging Potential. At this point your career is growing, and you are developing new skills. Decision-makers see your talent as a worthy investment of resources.

Solid Performer. You're comfortable with your talent, an above average performer, and could stay in this role, even until retirement, if all things remained the same. Decision-makers rely on the consistency of your brand promise.

High Potential. You've positioned your brand as one that is other and outer focused. You boost other's potential and seek ways to leverage systems to achieve organizational goals. Decision-makers are attracted to your tendency to offer new insights and come to expect your suggestions, perspectives, and high-level thinking.

Top Talent. Your brand is recognized as highly resourceful, industrious and collaborative. Growth in this sense is the expansion of your brand, like using 100% of your brain, you're using 100% of your talent. Decision-makers look for you to have a major impact on business results.

The target, the center of the chart, is reserved for that small pool of performers, found at all levels in an organization, who are the top performers and leading business contributors. These are the individuals who have marketable talent with the greatest amount of career leverage either within the same organization, by transferring to another organization, or even as an entrepreneur.

There is no time frame for progressing through this blueprint, and it is certainly not a race. Use it as a way to track progress and challenge yourself to move forward. Now let's take a closer look at the five areas that have the power to elevate your brand.

Measure the Five Levels of Your Brand's Impact and Influence

The impact you make and influence you have directly affects the emotional experience others have when they interact with your brand. Full disclosure here, the areas we are going to address might appear superficial – because in some ways they really are. In reality, it is difficult to separate your performance from the visual and interpersonal experience we have with one another. Every area listed here is "at play" in a decision-maker's choices in one way or another, and these areas are often the most overlooked aspect of how we manage our own brand.

To best gauge the type of impact and influence of our brand, we can look at those who embody the success we desire. Evaluate how those

---

Sarah Fisher, 26

Holder of the fastest qualifying time for a woman at the Indy 500 (four-lap average: 229.439 mph)

The biggest risk I ever took was when I walked away from Walker Racing in 2002. They wanted me to race the Atlantic Series in preparation for the Champ Car World Series. But I firmly believed in the Indianapolis 500 and helping the IndyCar Series grow to become the premier open-wheel series. I grew up dreaming about the Indy 500, and I wanted to contribute to that. I walked away from a solid job opportunity to make it on my own. I didn't have a job waiting for me but I said, "I'll find one," and I did.

–Interviewed by James M. Clash in 2007

individuals, often seen as high potential and top talent are presenting themselves within the organization. Taylor Swift, Misty Copeland and Steve Harvey are examples of role models, not just because of what they have achieved, but because of what they have experienced in life to reach their achievement.

How do your role models compare to your impact and influence at work and at play? This is the underlying key to organizational decision-making. Every organization wants top talent, and they want it packaged a certain way because that package represents the image the organization is trying to convey to its customers and/or clients.

Your job is to help decision-makers see your potential to do great things. Develop yourself in a way that gets you more yes's than no's in your career. My husband Ray, who played college football, often tells us stories of Coach Fisher who didn't know how Ray made such great plays as an Outside Linebacker, he just knew he could rely on Ray to make things happen. Whenever a critical play needed to be made Coach Fisher would call Ray over and say "Green, go make something happen out there!" and sure enough he did! That's how great decision-makers operate, they want you to make something happen. They know they need a win and are looking for those who they can call on to achieve their desired outcomes. Is this you?

What is the degree of your impact and influence? Let's look at each of these areas to find out:

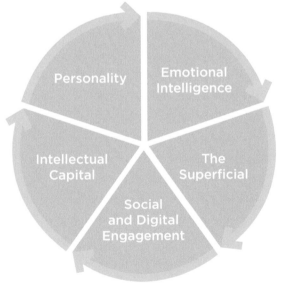

Emotional Intelligence

Do you control your emotions or do your emotions control you? Emotional Intelligence is our capacity to recognize, control and express our feelings or emotions and our ability to effectively handle our interpersonal relationships with others. In the model introduced by Daniel Goleman there are four main tenets to Emotional Intelligence:

1. Self-awareness: the ability to understand your emotions, recognize their impact, and use them to inform decisions.
2. Self-management: the ability to control your emotions and impulses and adapt to circumstances.
3. Social awareness: your ability to sense, understand, and react to the emotions of others within social situations.
4. Relationship management: your ability to inspire, influence, and connect with others, and to manage conflict.

There is no way to improve your behavior unless you know what makes you tick. Sound mental and emotional health are paramount to your career success; both depend entirely on your ability to understand why you behave the way you do. Your mental and emotional health are also dependent on your ability to effect changes if your behavior leaves something to be desired.

If you are unable to gain control over your behavior, you may find yourself repeating key life lessons before you can move in the direction you desire to take your life. This is a decisive element in the Brand Template and something I use in my coaching practice with clients.

Achieving self-awareness involves considerable self-exploration of our personality, values, and beliefs and how these impact our conduct, attitude and behavior. Having a better understanding of ourselves enables us to make powerful shifts that build on our strengths. As the first step to goal-setting, self-awareness is difficult to achieve if you don't know who you are. Knowing what you want therefore is difficult without knowing who you are. Seeking success is great provided you truly have the personality to cope with all its related pressures.

Being socially aware is about knowing how you react "in" and "to" social situations. Also, your ability to modify your interactions with other people to achieve the best results. Social awareness leads to the development and evolution of your social skills. To become more socially aware, you must learn to identify which types of situations make you uncomfortable, and then alter your behavior to make the best of your circumstances.

Managing your relationships with others must start with managing yourself. To be of greatest mutual benefit, relationships must not become stagnant, but instead enter a process of continual growth and development. A good working relationship means being proactive, addressing issues head-on, seeking resolutions, and searching for areas in which improvements can be made.

You will know you are engaged in well-managed relationships when you and others feel aligned, committed, on board and motivated. If you find yourself stuck, start with how you communicate.

Finally, we must take action where change is possible. This may not always be easy, especially when it relates to our own emotional shortcomings, but learning to adjust and control your emotions can lead to positive change.

The Superficial

This refers to all the things we don't like to discuss about ourselves in serious and meaningful ways but are often the culprits to career roadblocks. Superficial areas are rarely if ever mentioned by peers and supervisors or even family and friends. I'm referring to your weight, health, physical appearance, clothing and accessories, hair, make-up, cologne - you name it. That outer packaging that bleeps like a flashing warning light and can stop even the most talented person in their career tracks. Even qualified research supports the fact that your physical appearance plays a significant role in employment opportunities and career advancement to both advantage and disadvantage.

According to Workplace Psychology:

> *When making decisions about whether or not to hire prospective job applicants, interviewers are influenced by an applicant's attractiveness* (Shahani-Denning, 2003, citing Watkins & Johnston, 2000; Jawahar & Mattsson, 2005). *There is a great deal of evidence that being good-looking positively impacts the hiring decisions of employers* (Shahani-Denning, 2003, citing Watkins & Johnston). *This is known as the "what is beautiful is good" stereotype* (Shahani-Denning, 2003, citing Dion, Berscheid & Walster, 1972).

> *Kassin, Fein, & Markus* (2008, citing Hosoda, Stone-Romero, & Coats, 2003) *found that as a society, we tend to favor those who are good-looking. And while this isn't fair, research has found it to be true* (Watkins & Johnston, 2000).

Think about it, even if the contents of a can are good, no one wants to buy it if the can is dented – and if they do, they want it at discounted price. So it is with the superficial. We're not encouraging nose jobs and butt lifts, so please don't rush out for plastic or gastric bypass surgeries and say Pam Green sent you, but do make every effort to live a healthy lifestyle and put your best foot forward daily. If I were your career talent agent, I'd want you to get the full market value of your talent, so dig deep here.

"I do think that you can dress yourself out of a problem. The way that a haircut and a new pair of pants can make you feel is better than any therapist, because when you look in the mirror, you see a different person - you are a different person. It's superficial change that can lead to real change."

Greg Behrendt, comedian and script consultant to the HBO sitcom Sex and the City

If you believe there are no decision-makers who would allow superficial things to impact hiring you, then you're either lying to yourself, or you haven't lived long enough. I've worked with decision-makers who discriminate against candidates for unimaginable reasons, and trust me, they will not tell you the real reason; they just fall back on "not a good fit".

Consider this quote from a Cornell HR Review article:

> *"In short, attractive individuals will receive more job offers, better advancement opportunities, and higher salaries than their less attractive peers—despite numerous findings that they are no more intelligent or capable"*
> (Toledano, 2013, para. 5).

To get the full market value of your talent in the superficial, here's what you need to do to work your brand and reduce the possibility of rejection, so that your brand can work for you:

1. Get a head to toe physical. Dental, hearing, vision, physical and all the stuff in between. Being in good health should be a requirement for all of us and supports our desire to enjoy a long career.
2. Clean up your appearance. Iron your clothes, limit the cologne, and pay attention to dress requirements for your work – especially when with customers and clients. This includes grooming and personal hygiene.
3. Exercise regularly. At least 20 minutes per day to maintain strength, endurance and a healthy heart.
4. Eat healthy. See a nutritionist if you have to, but again, you will never perform at your optimal level if you are an unhealthy eater. Food has the power to bring us up or take us out. Every day you have the choice of which path you are following. Your physician can help you set achievable goals; work with him/her to do so.
5. Follow the instructions of your attending physician. If your physician says lose weight, quit smoking, reduce alcohol consumption, take your meds, drink more water, exercise daily...then just do it!!

I can only suggest, in a real way, proven strategies that can elevate your brand. If it weren't so, if I didn't experience it or see it first hand for myself, I would not call it to your attention.

The goal is to establish a personal style that complements your brand, fits within the dress code, and sets you apart from your peers. Your brand's clothing and accessories are essentially like a handshake following an introduction. If your handshake is weak – meaning you are not presenting a neat, clean and appropriately dressed outer appearance daily, it can send an unintended negative message and blind people to the talent you have to offer. However, if your handshake is firm – meaning, you are consistently dressed appropriately and aren't overpowering others with your cologne, perfume or lack thereof, you can send a very positive message.

Social Engagement

Social engagement is where you get to practice presenting your brand. Your social network is an interconnected group of people you find to be professionally supportive and helpful. When leveraged, they can help to advance your career and solve personal and professional challenges. Your resume used to shoulder the burden of conveying who you are along with what you could do. Today, your resume is like a postcard that invites an employer to check you out online. The invitation, your resume, should be great, don't get me wrong, but it is only a start. You can control how your brand is viewed by taking control over how you interact socially (in person) and digitally (social media and online).

> "Social media is changing the way we communicate and the way we are perceived, both positively and negatively. Every time you post a photo, or update your status, you are contributing to your own digital footprint and personal brand."
>
> **Amy Jo Martin, author**

LinkedIn is the non-celebrity's "Wikipedia". If you are considered a "professional" in your career you'll want to have an up-to-date profile in LinkedIn, one of the first places many employers go when in search of talent. Make sure your LinkedIn profile and professional photo are both current.

> TWEET THIS:
>
> **"LinkedIn is the non-celebrity's "Wikipedia". Are you in? #careers #branding #TLAB**

There are many limitations to what you can do in LinkedIn, so for this reason I suggest you also snag your own name as a .com or other related extension, and create a landing page or personal website that showcases your talent. This way when potential employers "Google" your name you can offer them more compelling reasons why you are the best candidate for their opportunity. Some of my favorites include: www.devonstank.com; www.jimramsden.com; www.kristagray.com; www.ellensriley.com; and www.tanmade.com.

There is a fine line between branding yourself for an employer and branding yourself as a business. If you don't want to raise eyebrows, you'll want to position any type of personal web page as an extension of Facebook and LinkedIn. Offer free tips and insights that showcase your intellectual capital in meaningful ways and refrain from selling items that could be viewed as competing with an employer's brand, needs, and priorities. You'll want your employer to see your personal web page as a way to help them achieve organizational success – while it boosts your visibility.

Beyond that, how do you leverage your brand beyond your resume and determine exactly where you need to establish and maintain a digital presence? That decision begins with knowing your audience. According to a report published by The Norman Lear Center, a nonpartisan research and public policy center that studies the social, political, economic and cultural impact of entertainment on the world, the U.S. "exports approximately $8 billion worth of entertainment product each year.... In 1999, the top four grossing movies at the international box office were Titanic, Jurassic Park, Star Wars: Phantom Menace, and Independence Day. Each of them made more money abroad than domestically, with Titanic earning more than twice as much overseas."

> "She treats her fans like friends, speaks their language, plays their games — all while encouraging their documentation of her album purchase."
>
> **Lindsey Weber, from the online Vulture article, "Taylor Swift is the Reigning Queen of Celebrity Social Media."**

To meet the needs of a growing global audience, film, music and broadcasting giants have had to establish their business presence internationally. This facilitates greater relationship building, an understanding of the global market's entertainment needs and establishes a framework for their work to be embraced by foreign audiences. Does Will Smith need to speak Mandarin to engage a Chinese audience that loves his films? No, his talent just needs to appeal to their entertainment needs. Likewise, your brand must appeal to those that need your talents, but first you need to get to know your audience of decision-makers.

To help you determine which social media sites, groups and organizations you need to engage, review the questions below. Get laser-focused so you can effectively target the specific audience in need of your talent.

- **Who** is my audience? Who are the individuals and organizations that are in need of or regularly hire someone with my talent?
- **Where** is my audience? What geographic locations do they populate? Where are they most active in social media? Where do they advertise for jobs?
- **What** associations does my audience support or engage? What causes are important to them?
- **How** are they being socially responsible?

As you build your digital profile, you'll want to connect with people in your audience - or who are connected to your audience. You'll do things like attend networking events, social hours, join Meet Up's and industry or professional groups and associations. You'll use those engagements to leverage your digital profile as an extension of who you are and what you can do. Having strong social and digital engagement practices has the effect of boosting your brand and your branding efforts.

Intellectual Capital

Your intellectual capital is what you know. Intellectual capital is to your career what a producer is to filmmaking. In order to create a successful film project, the producer has to be knowledgeable about the entire process of filmmaking from the introduction of the initial story idea and casting to filming, sound recording, editing and screening.

The producer isn't responsible for performing every role at every stage in the filmmaking process, though they must be keenly aware of the entire process from start to finish in order to know the extent to which a film project will be financially successful when released.

When actors seek to extend the life of their brand, they leverage their intellectual capital (knowledge of the filmmaking process) to make shifts in their careers to direct, write and produce. Likewise, you can use the knowledge you gain and competencies you develop through formal and informal training, development, and experiences to produce results and demonstrate value.

When you know how a business defines success and how the work impacts the company's growth and sustainability, you can enjoy significant career strides, develop multiple talents, and revel in career longevity.

Personality

Your personality exemplifies your conduct, attitude and behavior in speech, mannerisms, body language, conversation and overall experience others have with your brand. It is the outward expression of your mental, social and emotional wellbeing. To get the greatest mileage out of your career, your personality should be regarded as extremely positive.

Charlie Sheen, Mel Gibson, and Lindsay Lohan are shining public examples of people who have allowed their personality and perhaps other interferences to stifle their career potential. Our personality is what sets us apart from everyone else, making us attractive or unattractive in the eyes of the decision-maker.

The more attractive personality qualities we display, the more people want to be around us. Obviously the opposite is true for those whose personalities border on hostile or offensive. Although our personality is what defines us, and might not drastically change over time, through emotional intelligence, our behaviors can. When this happens you're not changing who you are, you're just making yourself more likable.

Taylor Swift epitomizes all five of these areas:

1. Her personality is described as "clever," "the real deal," and "driven."
2. She has been touted as the "Queen of Social Media" commanding more than 61 million follows on Twitter, over 40 million on Instagram, and holds a commanding presence in Tumblr, YouTube, and Facebook.
3. A student of the music business, the intellectual capital she is gaining is shaping her brand to be known as more than a singer-songwriter.
4. Taylor uses her music to express her self-awareness and her ability to understand those around her.
5. Taylor's public presence and persona are evidence that she is keenly aware that as superficial as it may seem, someone is always watching, evaluating and assessing her brand.

Recognize the importance of including all the key elements of your talent template, and refrain from resting on talent alone. To *Think Like A Brand*, you want everyone to say "yes" at every encounter they have with your brand. Yes - when they see you; yes - when they hear you; and yes - when they evaluate your brand. Every time you hear "yes", the value proposition of your brand has just increased!

Resist the Urge to Quit

During a tough moment of wanting to give up, here are the words my husband spoke to me,

"Pam, the thing that stops people most is not what's in front of them, but what's inside of them."

I was suffering and really wanted the attack to stop. The only way I saw that happening was to quit. After his words fitly spoken, I came to realize that we

> TWEET THIS:
> "The thing that stops people most is not what's in front of them but what's inside of them." #careers #branding #TLAB

must be able to take the assaults that impact our lives in order to fully appreciate the accolades.

I have yet to meet anyone who hasn't suffered something in this life; suffer the death of a loved one, suffer rejection, suffer pain, suffer loss of a job. Even in my own life, I have suffered. Could it be that in some strange way suffering is a means of preparing you for your destiny? If suffering weren't part of the process of *Thinking Like A Brand*, then perhaps the road on my Brand Map would be straight. But there are no straight roads to success. Have we not all suffered at some point in our careers?

Sometimes it seems the only answer to suffering in our careers is to quit. But for many of you reading this book quitting isn't an option. If that is the case for you, as it was for me, I had to change my thinking to reflect the fight that was inside of me. I took my focus off of people and put it on the goal by asking myself:

- If I must remain in this state of suffering for a season, then what am I learning about myself?
- What shift is suffering causing me to make in my conduct, attitude and behavior?
- What is the personal benefit of what I am enduring?

What I have come to realize during my seasons of suffering, especially when it appears the pain is being inflicted by other people and not by the circumstances themselves, is that my suffering is never about the other person. In fact, I've come to believe that other people are merely instruments being used to form and mold me like a potter's tool.

I remember having a challenging but successful run in a large global organization. It was challenging because of negative and hurtful things said to me by key decision-makers, marginalizing me to entice me to quit. The intense pressure and marginalization actually had the result of helping me strengthen my talent as a speaker, coach, trainer and strategic thinker.

On my last day of employment, I had a job offer and a consulting offer, and I've never looked back. The very thing my oppressors were afraid of is the very thing that I thrive on today. In this instance, my suffering was a signal that I was in the final stages of preparation for my next big thing. Just hold on, establish your strategy, reflect, rethink, shift, and most of all improve.

Fighters press forward in the face of adversity; that's what we do.

Chapter Summary

How do you "Taylor Swift" your brand?

1. **Build a reputation for excellence.** Master it, embrace it, showcase it and leave

decision-makers wanting more in such a way that they are willing to open new doors just for the opportunity to experience more of you.

2. **Seek to make an emotional connection** with key decision-makers, customers, teammates, and other important stakeholders. They will pick up your defense in trying times and push you forward.

When Taylor was criticized for her vocal performance during the 2010 Grammy Awards, it was industry veterans such as Stevie Nicks, and others who came to her defense. She went on to win countless honors that year including Time Magazines 100 Most Influential People in 2010, a year in which it was predicted this Grammy performance would "end her career overnight". Like Taylor's fans and supporters, when you face challenges, your supporters will pick up your defense in trying times, helping you to recover quickly and move forward with determination.

3. **Assess your brand's impact and influence.** These five areas could be the determining factor or detractor to your achievement. Taylor is a master in all f ive of these areas proving it can be done. But you don't have to be a superstar or have a manager, agent or publicist to tell you how to manage your brand's impact and influence. What you need is a healthy sense of self, people who will give you honest feedback, and the willingness to look around and learn from those who are doing it well.

4. **Resist the urge to quit.** I can't imagine the type of pressure that someone like Taylor Swift must endure, but I can empathize because there is pressure in every industry, in every organization in the world. Pressure can produce one of two things: 1) the desire to quit, or 2) the determination to improve. If you don't have inner tenacity, you won't have outer longevity.

You are the only one who will get to decide what you are remembered for, so, like Taylor Swift, design a brand template that is capable, credible, and competent, with marketable skills that enable you to scale your brand for an exciting career.

GROW STRATEGIC BRAND VISIBILITY

"You've got to find a way to make people know you're there."

Nikki Giovanni, author

Beyoncé

Singer, songwriter, actress, model, spokesperson and business woman

Beyoncé is a strategic brand. Though she is quoted as saying she does not like to think of herself as a brand, she does acknowledge that though she has multiple marketable talents, her focus is on leaving a legacy – that is what great brands do.

From her parents, she learned to give intentional effort to her brand even as a young woman. Being placed in private schools is intentional. Competing in talent shows at an early age is intentional. Forming a singing group is intentional. These intentional, consistent, and positive public expressions of Beyoncé, whether alone or with others, allowed her to build an audience that demanded more of her brand.

Beyoncé rose to fame as a lead singer with the 90's world famous girl group Destiny's Child. She received five Grammy Awards after the release of her first album, "Dangerously In Love", in 2003. Between the release of her first album and her highly publicized and celebrated marriage to rapper Jay-Z in 2008, she continued to perform, produce successful music, and started an acting career, debuting in the 2006 award winning film Dreamgirls.

On stage, Beyoncé's performances are unmatched, being celebrated as one of the best entertainers in contemporary popular music. With her 20 Grammy Awards (at this writing) she is the most nominated woman in Grammy history. She has received honors and awards from ASCAP, BET, MTV Movie Awards, American Music Awards, and Billboard Music Awards to name a few. In addition, she holds the Guinness World Record for the Fastest-selling iTunes Album of All Time.

Her strategic visibility has parlayed her into a number of business ventures including perfume, clothing, and music streaming. With sales over $400 million at this writing, the six versions of her Heat perfume are the world's best-selling celebrity fragrances.

It seems there is no end in sight for this hard working and highly celebrated business woman, whose consistent, intentional and positive display of talent makes her a perfect candidate for our fifth *Think Like A Brand* Secret:

SECRET #5:
Show Up. Speak Up. Demonstrate what you were born to do.

"Do what you were born to do, you just have to trust yourself."

Beyoncé

Confidence is one of the definitive elements required for sustaining success because confidence opens doors to visibility and the opportunity to do what you believe you were born to do. The confidence we have in ourselves is foundational to our performance, but I'm referring to the confidence we cause others to have in us, in our abilities, our talents.

When someone has confidence in you, it is likely because you have done something right, consistently, over a period of time. Your consistent delivery in your performance, your relationships, your attitude, conduct and behavior all paint a picture of the type of person you are for anyone who is watching.

When you perform in excellence, it is a form of showing up and speaking up. However in order to achieve some level of visibility, you will be required to take some risks:

- The risk that an idea might be rejected.
- The risk that there could be repercussions from decision-makers who aren't ready for or interested in your elevated contributions.

If you don't accept these as risks, fear could prevent you from obtaining the visibility needed to move your brand from one with potential to one with top talent.

> **TWEET WORTHY:**
> "One common factor among organizations worldwide is the need to more effectively understand and use their people's talents, skills, and energy."
>
> **State of the Global Workplace Report by Gallup**

It is the daily positive display of your brand, regardless of where you are and what you're doing, that can lead to new opportunities. The visibility of your brand, combined with your conduct, attitude and behavior can lead to new opportunities when you:

1. **Believe you have something to offer.** If YOU don't believe you have something to offer, it will show in your conduct, attitude and behavior. To boost your confidence, forget about being perfect and instead focus on your achievements and the positive affirmations about your talent.
2. **Present a genuine demeanor.** To be perceived as authentic and without pretense, learn to develop good listening skills; offer genuine compliments and when you must, speak the truth in love. Admit when you are wrong, and refrain from consistently judging others.
3. **Develop your talent.** Louis Pasteur famously said, "Chance favors the prepared mind," and when preparation meets opportunity, all the world is a stage for your Brand leading you to a broader and more satisfying career experience with multiple streams of income opportunities.

Show Decision-makers How To Leverage Your Talent

When you are hired for a job, if you do that job really well, you get to stay and keep doing that same thing year after year! What a comforting premise if that is what you want; what an easy formula to follow. But what if you find you can do other things that might be more fulfilling, then what?

In my early life, I worked for years in medical records and social work. I was not a licensed social worker, but I took every advantage of the growth opportunities these organizations offered. Still all the assignments were in medical records and social work. I was burning out quickly, and a degree in either line of work was not at all exciting for me.

Someone said to me that the best way to look for opportunities to leverage my talents was right where I was. I knew I was an excellent typist, I was extremely organized, had great relationships with others and was a fast learner among other things. So I positioned myself for a different internal opportunity. By following this thinking, I was soon promoted to Executive Assistant, which led to supervision, that led to board governance, and that led to a career in human resources.

I went from boredom and limited options to a challenging career at that same organization for more than nine years. That formula of showing up, speaking up and making my talents known, played well for me for the remainder of my career. I still benefit from this same formula today.

Opportunity #1: Show Up! Speak Up!

Instill confidence in your brand and take control of how you want to be viewed and perceived.

Have you ever wondered why you were passed over for a promotion or special assignment when it seemed apparent you had what it took to handle the job? Sometimes, it isn't that you don't have the talent, it is that decision-makers don't know enough about your talent because you aren't speaking up in meetings.

If you don't say anything, it might be taken that you don't have anything to contribute. There are many ways to speak up. I've always had a mind toward career advancement, and so I've made it a career practice to ensure that every interaction with decision-makers, executives, customers, and board members was positive. I looked for ways to be helpful and worked very hard to avoid saying "no" when asked to do things outside of my scope or comfort zone.

Many times when I was unsure about a particular request I'd lead with the sentence, "If someone will show me how, I'll give it my best shot". I'd work to finish assignments on time, ahead of time and on point! In addition, I'd speak up and share insights, observations and suggestions with decision-makers in person and in meetings.

I'd also look for ways to support another's point of view to build a path to credibility. The critical thinker that I am made that part difficult. I'd much rather distill an idea in a meeting to reduce the fluff than to go on incessantly about how great it is. To combat this urge, there are times I will turn what might be a criticism into a thought-provoking question while also offering solution-oriented ideas. Sometimes your brand is elevated not by showcasing what you know, but instead by helping those around you arrive at the best approach to a challenge.

Consider these thought provoking questions:

- What will be the impact of this decision on our customers, employees?
- What will be the short/long-term gains as a result of this move?
- What risks do we face in the short/long run as a result of moving in this direction?
- How will we measure success?
- Do we know what success should look like in three or six months?

You can add value to any conversation by not feeling you always HAVE to have the answer but by leading the individuals or members of your team to the answer that is best for the long-term sustainability and growth of the organization.

Opportunity #2: Make It About the Needs of Others

What do you need to be successful? This is a question that attracts decision-makers. This is a better question than asking, "What do you need from me?" or "How can I help you?" because the focus of these two questions is on you and not on them.

When people tell you how you can help them be successful, the door to learning new skills and opportunities to strengthen and showcase your talent can swing wide open.

Brand Visibility is optimized not by waiting to be discovered but by helping the organization recognize how to put our talent to extraordinary use! Here are some additional strategies to *Think Like A Brand* and get noticed at work.

Implement These Ten Strategies to Showcase Your Strategic Agility and Get Noticed At Work

Once your Brand Template is polished, you are ready for visibility. Brand Visibility, therefore, is one of the most dynamic aspects of *Think Like A Brand* because it requires action and moves from just thinking like a brand to acting like one. If you aren't able to embrace this stage, you'll find the remaining elements of our brand-thinking template difficult to execute. There are some pre-requisite requirements you'll want to adopt first:

- A reputation for delivering results.
- An attitude of excellence.
- Highly regarded conduct and behavior.
- Speak, only when you have something important to say, not just to say something.
- Stand clear of associating with people known to have poor reputations.

All of these standards will not only elevate your visibility but will also give a major boost to your credibility. Your goal is to eliminate the notion that you might not be ready for the next level. Adopt these behaviors and expect to get noticed:

#1 Break out of your shell, and maybe away from your posse!

Your posse, the group of friends or work associates you most interact with, is invested in who you are right now because you are a reflection of one another in a way that you enjoy. If you are only associated or "seen" to associate with this one group of homogeneous people, sometimes decision-makers will find it difficult to ascertain whether you can successfully engage people who are not reflective of your core group.

Challenge yourself to look for ways to broaden your circle. Not only will you increase your brand possibilities but there is also the likelihood you will broaden your mindset. The more of a worldview you have through experiences with other skillsets, abilities, cultures, backgrounds, etc., the more enriching you'll find your ability to connect with others and broaden your career opportunities.

#2 Improve Your Communication Skills

When you optimize your ability to communicate, meaning you skillfully and deliberately exchange information ensuring that your intended message is actually received, you are more effectively able to connect with peers, customers, and decision-makers, build trust and respect, and feel heard and understood.

One of the most important aspects of communication is becoming a good listener making certain you understand the intentions and emotions behind what is being said while also managing your own emotions and intentions.

When you develop a technique for listening, you'll find that it has the effect of also making you more attractive to be around. Good listeners have been found to:

- Write down the key points of a discussion or argument from the speaker's point of view so they understand what is being conveyed.
- Repeat back and summarize key points of a discussion before considering their own point of view.
- Make good eye contact while listening.
- Give the person speaking their full attention which has the effect of putting the speaker at ease.
- Intentionally adjust their communication style to complement the person with whom they are speaking.
- Make sure their facial expressions and body language convey positive signals to the person speaking (unfold those closed arms).
- Give themselves a few seconds to consider what has been said BEFORE responding.
- Do not interrupt the person speaking but instead wait to ask powerful follow-up questions to ensure to the speaker you really are listening.

However, having good listening skills is only part of communicating, there is still the issue of communication style. You can have good skills that reflect eye contact, repeating what you've heard, waiting for the other to finish their sentences, etc. while failing to complete the process of communication by developing a style that is genuine.

A good communication style refers to your mannerism, charisma and your presence. Good communicators are genuine listeners and consider the feelings and emotions of the person with whom they are speaking rather than rushing to make their point. They make themselves a little vulnerable by encouraging feedback on their suggestions and ideas. Being intentional about creating a positive impression, they are the ones at networking events who pull others into a conversation that may seem closed.

Adopting good communication habits can lead to fewer mistakes, shared learning, opportunities to collaborate, enhanced productivity, innovation and creativity, and improved satisfaction of both decision-makers and customers.

#3 Ask Powerful Questions

Joel Olsteen said, "You can change your world by changing your words." What if you could change how you are perceived and received just by asking well-positioned powerful questions? A question becomes powerful when it has the ability to motivate the action of others. While you should, of course, be prepared with answers to real business problems, sometimes having all the answers can make you appear like a know-it-all. In cases where you fear this might be true, look for opportunities to motivate change by asking questions that stimulate thinking on a deeper level. For example:

- What do we stand to gain/lose as a result?
- What effect will this have on our short/long- term goals?
- On a scale of 1-10 how would you rate this as a priority in the overall scheme of things?
- What have we already tried?
- What will happen if we keep doing this for the next five or ten years?
- Are we doing work that is aligned with our vision, mission and strategy?
- Is this one of our core competencies?

All of these questions and even more have the ability to shift you from feeling like you must have all the answers to creating an environment that will stimulate business breakthroughs right on the spot.

#4 Understand the Position of the Opposition

How can you add value if you don't know what the problem is? This requires that you know the business and the business frame of reference. If you're in HR, and the 'opposition' is in finance, perhaps the issue isn't you personally, but their frustration that your department doesn't appear to understand the bottom line, or is making poor financial decisions.

> **TWEET THIS:**
> **"There are two types of people in the world, those who have something to say and those who just have to say something." Plato #careers #TLAB**

A board member once shared this quote by Plato with me after a board meeting in which one of the board members was extremely negative and disruptive: "Pam, there are two types of people in this world, those who have something to say and those who just have to say something."

Now if the opposition appears to be purely personal, jump to #6 for additional insights.

#5 Look for Ways to Add Value

Adding value serves two purposes: 1) it keeps you in a positive frame of reference, and 2) it makes you more enjoyable to be around. These days, everyone seems to have an opinion and they don't mind sharing it. The negative effects are often the most obvious, but you can position a negative reflection in a positive light. For example:

"It appears we will not reach our sales goal this quarter; that is the bad news. The good news is that I may have uncovered some of the reasons why, and I even have a couple of suggestions for solutions."

If you tell a decision-maker what's wrong with something, my bet is that they already know because at least five others have already pointed out the problem. The dynamic completely changes if you provide a realistic and viable solution when you report the problem, not sometime later.

#6 Maintain an Unflappable Posture

This is an area I will work on for the rest of my life. Often referred to as knee jerk reactions, people are bound to do or say something that will push a button that opens the crypt to a dark side of yourself no one should ever see. Here are three ways to maintain control over your emotions:

- Identify and recognize your triggers. Sometimes just the presence of certain people, their posture and tone of voice can trigger an emotional reaction. Determine in advance how you will manage your interaction with them. Knowing that driving on the Beltway in DC opens the crypt, I often pray first, put on some calming music and either keep up with traffic or get out of their way.
- Choose your response. Many people don't realize that though the physiological reaction to emotional stimuli occurs in a matter of seconds, you can still choose how to react and respond. Project the outcome of a negative interaction and choose an alternative ending.
- Role model behind others who successfully manage their emotions. Early in my career I worked for a CEO, who had a board chair that seemed almost to hate him. The entire two years were brutal for everyone. I observed how unflappable the CEO remained during his interactions with this board chair, almost as if he had an invisible shield that made every unkind word bounce off of him. I asked the CEO how he did it, and he said, "I decided not to make him my focus and recognized our time would be short, to endure it and not give him what he wanted…to see me frustrated."

#7 Laser Speak

It seems that the human attention span gets shorter and shorter, seeming to look for information and communication to occur in 40 characters or less. Pay attention to the body language of people. They might not roll their eyes, but if you find you're getting cut off, avoided, or asked to "make it quick" more often than not, take note of these signals and consider how you share information. You might need to learn to speak more concisely and succinctly. Make your point and leave them asking for more.

#8 Improve Your Persuasive Power
To have the opportunity to do the things you want in your career, you'll need to persuade others of your talent and capabilities. If not, you'll find you are limited in your growth and career opportunities. So then, how does one improve their persuasiveness?

- Let your performance speak for itself. What exactly is your performance saying these days? It is saying that you are a consistently below average, average or consistently above average performer? Who wants to listen to advice from someone who isn't even performing at par?
- Build a reputation for a brand that delivers on time, on budget and with excellence.
- Align with the brand, needs and priorities of your organization. Being in alignment is understanding the direction of the organization and making sure your brand can keep up. Do your ideas and suggestions support you alone or do they support you and the organization's priorities?
- Paint pictures. Some studies suggest that 65% of the general public are visual learners, convey your message with word pictures and relevant stories to improve retention and the engagement of your brand.

#9 Learn To Laugh
Laughing disarms people and makes them less resistant to what you are saying. There is a difference, however, in interjecting a funny thought and in trying to perform stand-up comedy routines at every meeting. Which will be more positively persuasive?

#10 Be In the Moment
Give your undivided attention to what is being said and to the person in command of the floor. Behave as if you want to be there, not as if the meeting or conversation is an interruption to your day. Turn your anti-listening devices (cell phone, electronic tablets, music, etc.) to mute, give eye contact, and offer a posture that informs those in the room that you are fully engaged. Ask questions or offer input that demonstrate you really are there, in the moment, fully engaged and listening. This way, when it is your turn, you are more likely to receive a reciprocal response.

Survive A Brand Attack

Six Proven Methods
Beyoncé is not a brand without criticism. In fact, no brand can escape the occasional judgment, and sometimes the harsh review of their work from on-lookers, peers, customers, clients and decision-makers.

Not only did Beyoncé come under fire for performing a private concert for Libyan leader Muammar Qaddafi on New Year's Eve in 2010, she was also heavily criticized for appearing to lip-synch a pre-recorded version of "The Star-Spangled Banner" during the outdoor ceremony of President Barack Obama's second inauguration in January 2013 in Washington, D.C.

There are any number of reasons why you can find yourself on the defensive end of what feels like a personal attack. Sometimes people attack because you have in fact made a mistake – the bigger and more public, often the more intense the attack. Other times you come under fire simply because someone doesn't like you or what you represent. Still there are times the criticism is friendly fire – someone who is more comfortable with the way you used to perform or a prior role you filled and isn't interested or perhaps capable of supporting the "new" more progressive you. An attack can also be an issue of cognitive dissonance - you have introduced a thought or a concept that interrupts their worldview.

In an article by Sharon Ede *Surviving Personal Attacks – A Guide for Change Agents* she writes:

> *"...their view of the world is suddenly interrupted and made uncomfortable by new information or ideas that conflicts with their established understanding and belief system. The reaction is because your message has clashed with an individual or group's 'belief grid', or challenged values they hold dear."*

Any time a person or group of people feel the ideas they hold dear are questioned or challenged, they may respond in a negative way. You can have the best of intentions, and the best ideas, full of potential to move people, projects and programs forward exponentially, but the mere introduction of something new can bring out the worst in people; simply because they don't want to change their thinking or their behavior. So, what happens? They attack.

Sometimes the attack is passive aggressive, a hidden resistance to something you want to move forward while making it appear they are on board and supportive. Other times the attack is direct and personal where you or your ideas are called out and challenged in very public, negative ways such as in person, meetings, e-mail and even in social media.

We all handle harsh criticism differently. Beyoncé donated her fee from the Qaddafi performance to victims of the Haitian earthquake, fired her father as her manager, and refused to publicly address the presidential lip-synch controversy. But what can you do to survive a brand attack? There are at least six strategies you can adopt:

Recognize that there are some people who aren't going to like you, just because they won't like you. The more you do to challenge the status quo, the more progressive you are in your career, the more you grow and develop for the better, the greater the resistance you are likely to face because of your disruption to someone's world view or even personal view about you. Try to strategize ahead of time how you'll respond to the introduction of a new idea or concept and do so in a positive manner.

Research the opposing view. The best defense is a great offense. When you are pitching a new idea or know you are introducing a concept that will require a shift in behavior and thinking, expect opposition and even some attack. But first prepare by knowing the position of the opposition. I recall having one leader that would attack me if I opened my mouth to sneeze so I learned to poll him ahead of time on his view of a new concept. He never disappointed and often offered harsh personal critique. This helped me prepare for his promised public attack where I was able to quickly address his and other's concerns and confidently move forward.

Resist the urge to launch a counter-attack and instead re-direct the focus of the attack to capitalize on your strengths. If you're attacked in a meeting, then focus on and accentuate the positive outcomes of the challenge; avoid launching your own defensive attack. Use facts and data as evidence to support your recommendation and direction. If you or others have experienced success in this area before, point to those outcomes as well. Stay in your zone, address the concern and use a little humor to settle the tension in the room.

Show **Reserve** and acknowledge shortcomings. When you humble yourself and acknowledge imperfections as well as successes, you demonstrate how more connected you are to those who criticize you than you are opposed. We all make mistakes and if one is pointed out, acknowledge it and how you have, are or will overcome. After all, is it better to be in a boat with a captain who has overcome a sinking ship or a captain who has no experience with the threat of defeat?

Remind people of why you are an asset. Remind them of why you are the best person to be in the stated position or why you were selected to lead the team for example. Saying things such as, "Besides, I believe the reason you hired me was…" or "The reason I was selected to lead this team…" are statements that help to demonstrate you do have talent worthy of their time and investment. Beyoncé, Michael Strahan, Taylor Swift and our other celebrity brands remind us daily of why they are worthy of celebration.

Remain positive. This is admittedly tough to do, but you can do it if you stay focused on the original positive intent of what you really want. Ask for mentoring from someone you know has endured a similar type of criticism. Adopt positive self-talk – you are an asset, and you do add value. Accept responsibility if it is warranted – but above all, learn to move on and refuse to be held captive by negativity.

Sometimes you can be right when defending yourself against a brand attack and still be wrong if you use the same weapons in battle that your attackers do.

Improve the positive impression of your brand by rising above the call to battle by those who intend more harm than good. Your weapons are rooted in fact and data, your track record for success and a consistent positive experience with your brand.

Chapter Summary

How do you "Beyoncé" your brand?

Brand Visibility directly builds off of a strong Brand Template. To capitalize at the Visibility stage requires you to speak up, make sure your voice is heard, that your brand exudes confidence and is respected. From there you can show the company how to take advantage of your talent in meaningful ways:

1. Trust the strength of your talents and develop confidence. Beyoncé is famous for saying that she is very shy and not at all like the brand we see on stage. Her ability to show up and speak up is a credit to her ability to push past her shy demeanor. It makes her intriguing and gives us strength to know we, too, can bolster our confidence if we believe we have something to offer.

2. Beyoncé continues to show entertainment and business executives how to leverage her talent in film, endorsements, and other business deals that align with her goals as well as theirs. When there is an alignment of goals, and you look for ways to showcase your brand, you and your organization can find success.

3. Look for ways to meet the needs of other people. Beyoncé has a strong female following who not only love the message in her music but who connect with her in a real, genuine way. She extends her connection to her audience through other business ventures including clothing and perfume. How are you meeting the needs of others? When your goals align with the brand, needs and priorities of the organization, you will begin to see how you really are meeting both your needs while also meeting the needs of others.

4. If your brand ever comes under attack, take a humble approach to how you view and respond to your critics. What we learn from Beyoncé is that it is ok to address a critique of your performance, but it is not ok to have to do so over and over and over again. Acknowledge mistakes and when you move on, so will others.

When you believe you have something to offer, are genuine in your dealings with others, and deliver excellence in your work, you'll experience the career satisfaction and longevity you desire. The true power of Thinking Like A Brand is really acting like one.

IDENTIFY YOUR BRAND ADJACENCIES

"You know, God gave me a gift to do other things besides play the game of basketball."

LeBron James, basketball player

Steve Harvey

Businessman, comedian, radio personality, actor, author, television host, mentor

Steve Harvey began his career performing stand-up comedy in 1985. Homeless for multiple years in the 1980's, he took odd jobs with the help of friends to sustain him while he continued to pursue his love of comedy. His big break came when he was a finalist in a national comedy search in 1990. This brand-defining moment led Steve to his long-running role as host of Showtime at the Apollo. Steve's command of comedy on stage transferred to a starring television role and to becoming the host of his own show for six years on the WB network.

Steve continued to use his marketable talent in comedy to transition to film, radio and other television roles such as becoming the host of The Steve Harvey Morning show in 2000, Family Feud in 2010 and a remarkable return to daytime television in a program titled Steve Harvey! Author of several critically acclaimed books including "Act Like a Lady, Think Like a Man", and the book "Straight Talk, No Chaser: How to Find and Keep a Man", he has parlayed his pension for advising men and women on dating into a dating site for women, called Delightful in 2014!

Steve's awards include three Daytime Emmy Awards and an impressive eleven NAACP Image Award wins in various categories! In addition he has received numerous honors including BET's Humanitarian Award, People's Choice Award, and Radio and Record's Magazine Personality/Show of the Year! This makes Steve a phenomenal example of our sixth *Think Like A Brand* Secret:

SECRET #6:
Marketable and transferable talent is what gives you career security and mobility.

"Your mission, your purpose and your destiny will all be tied to one thing – your gift."

Steve Harvey

Talent gets you the job. Transferable talent keeps you in the market. What's interesting about Steve Harvey is that Steve has had careers in boxing, insurance sales, carpet cleaning and postal services, but none were his passion, although all have elements of marketability and transferability. His continual passionate pursuit in the

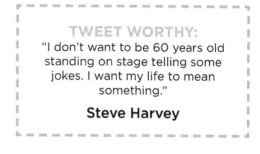

comedy arena forced him to improve his talent so he could enjoy the maximum market value of his brand. Steve's excellence in comedy opened doors for his exploration into many new business opportunities.

Talented people find jobs. Multi-talented people with marketable transferable skills find success. Steve Harvey found jobs, but comedy was more than a job, comedy was his talent, speaking was his talent, and people skills was his talent. The more related your talents are, the more interconnected they are, the easier it will be for you to maintain your brand.

What talents are you not using that could cause you to be more marketable or more valued by the company or in the open market? What talent might be transferable to another aspect of work in the field? This step helps you to look beyond your current situation and really assesses the value of your brand more broadly. Do you know the competitive value of your brand and your career potential? How far can you go in this or an adjacent line of work? What resources (people and financial), collaborations, and networks are necessary to boost your brand value and explore adjacent career options?

When you have talent you are capable of doing what everyone else does, find a great job or deliver a great service. When you have marketable and transferable talent, you increase the sustainability and longevity of your brand because you now have options for the direction of your career that didn't previously exist. Remember, talent will get you a job, but marketable transferable talent transcends time!

Engage These Eight Actions to Make Your Talent Transferable

Transferable talent is the collective presentation of your skills, strengths, capabilities and aptitude developed through education, life or work experience that you can apply to a variety of career opportunities. In Step 3 during your Brand Research, you determined there is a market for your talent and have sized that market. Now, in your journal I want you to write your answers to these questions from both a personal and professional perspective to determine transferability:

- What do people come to me for?
- What do I get called on to do the most?
- What do I like to do?
- What am I skilled at doing?
- What do I get paid to do?
- What do I love doing so much that I'd almost do it for free?
- What are the skills and capabilities I've developed that are still useful to me today?

The more willing you are to share and showcase your talent, the more likely transferability will be for you in your career. Transferable skills are easier for a current employer to see and experience than for an external employer. Try to experience transferability where you are before seeking to do so with a new employer, who might not be willing to take the risk.

First, get at the core of what you do.

All of us have been guilty of this: we look at a job title and think we know exactly what the person does or what the job entails. But a customer service representative in one organization could have almost entirely different types of responsibilities in another. Stop focusing on the title and focus on the core of the job. What is the core responsibility that leads to the ultimate outcome for the majority of the work you do? For example:

Recruiters: their core responsibility is to sell the company and source top talent. The ultimate outcome is to hire highly productive individuals that can boost the bottom line.

Customer Service Representative: their core responsibility is to build and retain satisfied customers. The ultimate outcome is to get the customer to make repeated purchases.

Collections Representative: their core responsibility is to recover delinquent funds owed to a company. The ultimate outcome is to maintain the company's profitability.

Human Resource Professional: their core responsibility is to maximize employee performance. The ultimate outcome is the achievement and success of tactical and strategic business objectives.

It does not matter if the level is entry or senior for each of these job types, the core purpose is basically the same. How they achieve the expected outcome is where employment levels come into play. When we get to the core of the job's responsibility, you can help current and potential employers see how your talent, not the title, is transferable.

Second, know the pain points of the employer.

This requires you to know something about the business and how a particular job impacts the business. Often the business implication is alluded to in the job title and other times it is written in the description or posting. For example, this posting is for an administrative officer:

"Wealth advisory firm is experiencing EXPLOSIVE growth and is in need of an Administrative Officer who will assume responsibility for maintaining and elevating the existing "client care" culture of our firm as well as the day-to-day operations. Our clients are "Raving Fans" and we want to keep it that way."

From this posting, we see that their pain points are rapid growth and the need for someone who can help them maintain highly satisfied customers in the transition. When information is this explicit, you'll want to specifically address how you can mitigate their concerns about you as a candidate for hire or promotion. This also requires you to get focused and crystal clear on your direction in your career resume, otherwise, you end up looking like you're job hopping and directionless.

Third, assess if you have the talent to address their pain points.

Is there something you're doing that you can tweak or change? Will your shift require further training, education or development, and if so will the company have to pay or are you willing to prepare yourself ahead of time?

Some career shifts simply can't be accepted by an employer without the experience to back them. This is an experience challenge. How does your experience transfer from one job to another opportunity? Don't assume you can make the jump from customer service representative to marketing manager if you don't have the education, experience and talent to back it up.

Go back to your Brand Plan and revisit your research. Does it answer the question, "Which companies need people like me?" You must get focused and be realistic about the types of jobs and careers that are aligned to someone with your experience. Employers prefer to recruit talent able to get up to speed relatively quickly and with minimal investment on the employer's part. The employer is going to look at the whole of your experience in less than one minute, if it doesn't make sense to them on the surface, you could get passed over. Make the connection make sense. Be realistic.

Fourth, know that people buy benefits.

How can your talents benefit the decision-maker? Write down all the ways in which your talent can benefit an employer and make it a key element in your Brand Plan. Some of the outcomes employers ultimately want include:

- Increased productivity
- Solution to an obvious business problem
- More productive (or even reduced) meetings
- Engaged individuals and teams
- Metrics and measures
- Alignment and clear expectations
- Sound policies, procedures and systems
- Improved safety protocols
- Established roles and responsibilities
- Innovation and creativity

When you think of selling the benefits of promoting, hiring or bringing you into a project or adding you to a team, some of the benefits could include:

√ Improved meeting productivity
√ Alignment of work to strategic business outcomes
√ Improved employee satisfaction and retention
√ Reduced waste
√ Reduction in slips, trips and falls
√ Reduced verifiable breakdowns in customer engagement
√ Reduced breakdowns in equipment failures
√ Increase in customer satisfaction and retention
√ Increase in promotable employees

These are just suggestions in how to turn your achievements into benefits for your current or future employer. Be prepared to answer the question, "How did you do that?"

Fifth, for both internal and external opportunities, demonstrate how your marketable transferable skills meet the job requirements but also address their pain points in writing.

Below is an example of a chart you can drop into your cover letter to help a hiring manager see clearly how your talent addresses the requirements of the job:

Your Requirements	My Experience
BS; SPHR and/or Advanced Degree	BS in Business/HR; MBA; SPHR Certified
10-15 Years Generalist HR Leadership	17+ years Generalist HR Leadership
Strong business acumen, well-honed communication and management skills, and experience working remote locations and service centers.	Managed $37m in Revenue, 25 staff (10 field offices); accustomed to more than 65% travel.
Private and/or family-owned company experience.	Successfully worked for a family-owned company.
Board and Executive Committee interaction.	Have 8 years board management experience, served on several community boards, served as HR staff liaison for Governing boards.
Experience taking a company public.	Experience establishing and running a for-profit organization.

This can quickly help the decision-maker see clearly how your talent aligns with their current opening and prevents them from digging through your resume in search of "fit". In fact, most will not take the time to dig and your qualifying experience could go unnoticed.

Sixth, leverage your digital footprint.

This of course speaks in part to your credibility and visibility. When you put yourself out as someone who can do certain things, then your digital footprint has to align with that. Your personal web page, and posts to Slideshare, Twitter and Facebook, etc. should include content that supports your knowledge base and frame of reference.

When actors and actresses want to be considered for film roles, they petition everyone connected to the project, they remain visible in the public eye, ensure their behaviors are aligned with their brands and don't just leave their brand in the hands of their manager and publicist. SPEAK to your audience and they will find you. Comment on posts that are aligned with your thinking. Don't make it difficult to follow what you're doing. You can use social media to build your credibility in areas you want to be known for, not just for areas where you have current expertise.

Seventh, volunteer your transferable talent to gain valuable experience.

Identify volunteer opportunities both externally and internally that would help you get valuable and credible experience in the adjacent field and establish a footprint for understanding that line of business.

Studies show that volunteering can boost job opportunities. In fact, according to the "Volunteering as a Pathway to Employment Report" by the Corporation for National and Community Service:

- Volunteers have a 27 percent higher likelihood of finding a job after being out of work than non-volunteers
- Volunteers without a high school diploma have a 51 percent higher likelihood of finding employment

In addition, volunteer for assignments no one wants but for which you have the talent to perform. Serious about making a change that furthers your goals? Then volunteer as a path to your success.

Eighth, seek transfer and promotional opportunities where you are. One of the easiest ways to showcase your transferable talent is to obtain a promotion or lateral job move. This shows a potential employer that you are quite capable of meeting new challenges and are willing to make your talents available to help the company achieve its goals.

All eight of these strategies are ways to showcase the transferability of your marketable talent. If none of these strategies work for you, then assess if your talents are marketable and if they are showing up as your strengths. If you are interested in broader and more diverse career opportunities, then let's discover your Brand Adjacencies.

Identify Your Brand Adjacencies

Brand Adjacencies are the potential ways in which you can create broader and more diverse career options. Not to be confused with growth opportunities which are progressive career advancements, such as moving from assistant, to manager, to senior manager, director and above in the same or similar field of work. Adjacencies seem to naturally evolve as a result of your collective life and work experiences and create opportunities to extend the life of your brand, thus shifting you to a more innovative and customized career path.

The result of identifying your potential adjacencies has the power to exponentially lift the value, visibility and credibility of your brand. Your adjacent success, however, is dependent upon your ability to operate from a place of excellence and authenticity. In other words, if your brand doesn't have a reputation for superior performance, will the lack of credibility support your exploration into broader opportunities?

Examine the experiences of a Restaurant Manager:

- Recruit and retain staff
- Foster a positive customer experience
- Oversee cash management
- Scheduling talent
- Vendor management
- Store maintenance
- Maintain high quality assurance standards

The successful restaurant manager receives high marks for performance and develops a reputation for excellence. Continued success leads to a credible, capable and competent brand, opening the door to a number of adjacent career options including:

- Establish a **training** program for restaurant managers
- **Write** books and training manuals about restaurant management success
- Become a motivational **speaker** on success in the restaurant business
- **Consult** on recruitment, retention, and restaurant management strategies
- Become known as a restaurant turnaround guru through **social media** activities
- **Coach** struggling restaurant managers
- **Teach** hospitality courses at local colleges and universities
- **Purchase** a franchise

Just as adjacent angles share a common side and a common vertex but do not overlap, so it goes with your Brand Adjacencies. From the experience described above, this person's success as a Restaurant Manager provided intellectual capital (knowledge) of restaurant management which profited him as a Franchise Owner. Brand Adjacencies utilizing shared knowledge and expertise provide real potential for multiple career or volunteer positions.

As you can see, depending upon other personal, volunteer and professional experiences, one could keep going with this list. Working for a different restaurant doesn't qualify as adjacent because the type of work hasn't changed, just the location. What makes the work adjacent is the alignment of overlapping knowledge and the collective complement of your successful career experiences.

This evaluation and exploration into the capabilities of your brand is what creates sustainability, longevity, and long-term profitability in your career.

Three points to keep in mind:

First is the success of your brand. If you don't carry a reputation for excellence, then the credibility of your brand could take a hit when looking to reach into adjacent opportunities.

Second, you can have a reputation for excellence but work for a tarnished organizational brand. Leverage this once you leave the organization using various forms of communication to teach decision-makers "what not to do".

Lastly, if you have made a criminal mistake, were convicted and served time for a crime, look for ways to "Frank Abagnale" your brand. Frank was convicted and served time in three prison systems (Swedish, French and US) for forgery, fraud and swindling. He is known as the most notorious impostor ever for crimes committed between the ages of 15 and 21. Today, almost 70 years old, he has spent the last 40 years as a securities consultant, advising and consulting with hundreds of financial institutions, corporations and government agencies around the world. He has also been the subject of films, books and a Broadway musical.

Not a push for glorifying crime, and certainly there might not be movies and Broadway musicals written about your exploits, but if you've made an authentic turnaround, consider how you can use your experiences to the benefit of someone else.

As you will see, there are multiple ways in which you can extend the life of your brand. Your set of adjacencies will be unique to your experiences. Here are a few examples of how adjacencies can be created:

Central Adjacency	Related Adjacencies				
Educator	Trainer	Speaker	Advocate	Activist	Teacher
Consultant	Advisor	Counselor	Mentor	Therapist	Coach
Performance Art	Dance	Comedy	Theatre	Music/ Singing	Film
Visual Art	Photography	Sculpture	Paintings	Drawings	Fashion
New Media Art	Video	Webinar	Blogs	Websites	Social Media
Literary Art (written work)	Novel	Fiction & Non-fiction	Short Stories/ Comic Books	Textbooks and Workbooks	Training Books

This list is not exhaustive. Once you have selected an adjacency to explore, you can extend your brand further by addressing the specific needs of a particular group based on age, race, gender, ability, ethnicity, social status, religion, etc. For example, Oprah Winfrey, an advocate for women and girls, has an all-girl school in South Africa. She crosses racial, ethnic, socio-economic status, age and gender boundaries to meet the needs of these young women.

Learn From My Brand Plan

My passion for helping people achieve personal and professional success coupled with my analytical skills, ability to be detail oriented, and rules-focused, led me to a career in Human Resources. My career experience plus the exposure of running an association expanded my view of the career potential and possibilities for someone with my talent. Based on this and the collective experience of my brand, I identified my **natural adjacencies** below:

- Educator
- Coach
- Facilitator
- Trainer
- Entrepreneur
- Author
- Speaker
- Consultant

My **desired adjacencies**, things I'd like to do given the opportunity, fall in these three categories:

- Television Programming
- Radio Programming
- Performance Art

There are no guarantees that my natural adjacencies will be any more successful than my desired adjacencies. The only difference is, a transition through my natural adjacencies will feel more comfortable and the ease of transition will feel more effortless and less strenuous than trying to transition into my desired adjacencies, simply because of my lack of exposure in these three areas.

What I did when I left my employer was play with my natural adjacencies. I sought work in as many of them as possible. I determined that I would settle only in the areas where:

1. I found professional and personal satisfaction
2. I experienced or could build a financially supportive customer base
3. There was real possibility, opportunity and demand for what my brand had to offer

It was only after a few years of testing that I settled on building a brand around coaching, speaking, writing, training and development, which gave birth to my current business venture.

Exploring your natural adjacencies will help you identify all the possible career tracks your brand can take, and the creative ways you can leverage your brand full-time, part-time, in volunteer roles and entrepreneurially.

Assess Personal Risk

It is exciting to think of all the potential ways to extend your brand. For those working in organizations, look for growth and development opportunities within the organization before seeking external experiences. And if you do seek external development experiences, make sure that any outside opportunities related to the development of your brand do not present a conflict of interest with the work you are performing for your current employer.

While more and more organizations are making it less difficult for high-performers to have a "side hustle", you'll want to read your organization's internal policies and speak with someone in human resources before seeking to extend your brand in related areas outside of work.

Be Realistic About Money, Power and Influence

What I am sharing in this book is an approach an average person can take to enjoy career success and longevity. These strategies are what I have learned from those in various industries who have extended their careers through the creative expression of their brand.

The difference between you, me and the Jay-Z's and Oprah's of the world: these highly influential and financially secure brands have achieved the status and money to cross boundaries and venture into unique territories more than the average person reading this book.

If Oprah wanted to create a perfume line, or Richard Branson, designer clothing, they very well could with little regard to adjacencies. And though alignment with brand recognition is important, they can afford to take a greater risk.

Most of us don't have infinite resources, so we have to be thoughtful and strategic about how to invest our time and money. We also have to be realistic about our brand's natural adjacencies. If you aspire to move into unique territories then make sure you have the credibility, competence, resources, know-how, finances, and support to reach and build an audience that will support a risky move. Otherwise, look for ways to align what you want to do with the reputation you are building now. If you really wish to venture into adjacencies that are not seemingly a natural fit, then take the time to build your brand capability, credibility and competence before doing so.

Neither money nor desire is a guarantee of success. However, money makes you better able to rebound from your mistakes and desire gives you the motivation to keep trying.

Chapter Summary

How do you "Steve Harvey" your brand?

Marketable and transferable talent leads to brand sustainability. It doesn't mean you'll never get fired, downsized, or reorganized, but it does mean that regardless of the impact of organizational shifts, you'll have realistic career alternatives for the long-term sustainability of your brand.

Steve Harvey teaches us that the expression of your gift is directly tied to your mission, your purpose and your destiny. Being in hot pursuit of your destiny will require you to do the following things to see your goals realized:

1. **Practice The Eight Ways to Make Your Talent Transferable**
   Transferable talent is the collective presentation of your skills, strengths, capabilities and aptitude developed through education, life or work experience that you can apply to a variety of career opportunities. The core of the Steve Harvey brand is comedy. You can expect to laugh during every engagement with Steve. It also happens to be a strength that is highly marketable and in demand. What he does really well is identify the pain points of his audience in every venture whether it is his talk show or his dating website. He knows his audience well and he is producing content and creating experiences that meet their needs.

2. **Identify Your Brand Adjacencies**

   Brand Adjacencies are the potential avenues through which you serve your life's purpose and elevate your message. Adjacencies seem to naturally evolve as a result of your collective life and work experiences and create opportunities to extend the life of your brand. What we learn from Steve Harvey is that as a comedian Steve knew that comedy was not the only avenue for expressing his brand. He repeatedly tested the limits of his brand by exploring adjacencies that naturally aligned with comedic talent. He explored television, comedy tour, radio, film and books to name a few. Test the boundaries - explore creative instinctive ways to extend the life of your brand.

3. **Learn From My Brand Plan**

   I promised no-fluff, real practical ways to *Think Like A Brand*. I'm the living test, having watched many sports, entertainment, business and arts brands follow this blueprint, I saw an opportunity to conduct my own real world test. If a man, once homeless, can rise to the level of success as Steve has, then it was worth the risk and I am proof positive it works.

4. **Assess Personal Risk**

   Steve, like other sports, entertainment, business and arts brands make it look very easy. Truth is, building a sustainable brand is hard work. It requires research, personal investments of time and money and still there are no guarantees. What we learn from Steve and other brands is that not everything you do will be loved by 100% of the people. It is also wise to mitigate the risks of conflict of interest by knowing the rules around part-time jobs and other activities by speaking with your current employer.

5. **Be Realistic About Money, Power and Influence**

   These are strategies taken from some of the best and brightest in sports, entertainment, business and art. While most didn't start out with a silver spoon in their mouths, what we can learn from Steve and others is to be money smart. Michael Strahan did his homework and realized that if he didn't scale his brand, he too could be broke within two years of leaving the NFL. Steve refused to return to a homeless state and reinvested in profitable ventures that align with his brand. Money makes it easier to take the kinds of risks that wealthy people sometimes take. If you don't have that kind of money, make your risks a little more calculated. Make sure your *Think Like A Brand* Map aligns with your talent and is realistic while also sensible.

SCALE YOUR BRAND

"I believe excellence is being able to perform at a high level over and over."

Jay-Z, music mogul

> To scale your brand is to demonstrate behaviors that ensure you deliver consistent performance over time at a high level, resulting in upward career mobility and sustainability.

Sara Blakely

Entrepreneur, businesswoman, and philanthropist

With a vision, $5000 in personal savings and a goal to design a comfortable undergarment that did not show beneath her white pants, Sara Blakely has transformed her pain point into a billion dollar enterprise.

Following graduation from college with a Bachelor's Degree in communications, like most of us, Sara set out to pursue her professional career. She started out at Disney and after three months landed a door-to-door sales job that lead to a promotion as a national sales trainer. At every leg of her journey, Sara was strengthening her talent.

In 1998, Sara ran into a snag, quite literally. While working as a national salesperson for a large international imaging and electronics company, Sara found that her traditional pantyhose provided a flattering control top, but the band was uncomfortable, and the foot seam with open toed shoes simply wasn't working for her. In an instant, she cut off the feet of her pantyhose and realized she had stumbled upon an invention that might be appealing to other women as well. Spanx undergarment for women was born.

While continuing to work her full-time job over the two-year process, Sara, devoted much of her non-work hours to exploring her adjacent talent through the research and development of her product. After enduring many rejections from the male-dominated hosiery manufacturing industry who failed to see her product's value, she ultimately found a factory to produce her product idea.

With limited dollars, Sara used her talent to complete her own patent application, and manage the advertising of her product herself, which included presenting and modeling to boards and buyers of large store brands including Neiman Marcus. This exposure also opened the door to sales with Bloomingdales and Saks 5th Avenue.

Two years and thousands of hours later, her hard work and ability to leverage her talent pays off when Spanx are featured on the television show Oprah, as one of Oprah Winfrey's Favorite Things for 2000. Popularity and sales of the Spanx brand went through the roof.

Today, Blakely, the youngest self-made female billionaire in the world, has graced the cover of many magazines and has been featured on numerous television programs. She retains 100% ownership of Spanx, and because of her ability to leverage her talent in communications and sales, she has never had to use formal advertising. Sara's ability to leverage her entire life experiences towards the achievement of her goals, from vision and mission to research and brand visibility to sustainability, makes her the perfect living, breathing example of what it means to *Think Like A Brand* and a perfect reflection of Secret #7:

SECRET #7:
Visualize where you're headed, giving your time and effort to growing your capabilities, credibility and competence.

"I think very early on in life we all learn what we're good at and what we're not good at, and we stay where it's safe."

Sara Blakely

Scalable brands do not play it safe. If it is a promotion you're after, or some higher level of achievement, like others who've attained a higher level of success, you too must learn to think on the level of your promotion and not on the level of your comfort zone. A higher level of thinking requires vision, determination and risk. Sara Blakely possessed all three.

In football, there is a play called the timing pattern in which the QB doesn't throw to the player but throws to a spot. The receiver's job is to get to the spot where the ball is to arrive, catch the ball and head for a touchdown. This move by the QB is a risky one. It requires judgment and the ability to see where things should be and not solely on where they are. If you rest in the place where it's safe, with no room for risk or failure, how will you ever achieve your goals?

> **TWEET THIS:**
> "Learn to think on the level of your #promotion and not on the level of your comfort zone." #careers #branding #TLAB

Your job right now, today is to build a brand that positions you to receive an opportunity that your employer is working towards and to be prepared to catch it when the time arrives. Don't focus on staying where you are, instead place your focus on where you want to be, while developing your talents right where you are.

Sara successfully accomplished two things: 1) she continued to produce at a high level for her employer, while also 2) using her talent to develop a product that led her toward the type of achievements she could only dream of.

Learn the Culture

Mastering the basic elements of your job begins with doing the job well, and includes your engagement with those around you - those whose opinion of you and your work matter. Mastering the basic elements of your job and doing that well, like Sara Blakely, can and often does lead to greater exposure and additional talent building opportunities.

On average it can take a year to learn the players and personalities found within an organization and for you to experience the culture through cyclical periods. That cycle often starts over when new leadership takes over. In order to get to the place where you can think on the level of your promotion, you must give yourself some time to understand the culture of growth, development, business practices, etc. in the organization.

Look for what happens when leaders take notice of high potential talent. What happens when someone falls from grace? How are decisions made and who are the chief decision-makers? What are the rewards for doing well, and what happens when the organization (and individuals) perform poorly?

When you learn the organization's culture, you learn how things get done. Then you get to decide: Is this the type of culture where you will find professional success or is it a stepping-stone to other things?

Engineer the Use of Your Brand

Brand engineering is planning how you want to be perceived and engaged by decision-makers, peers and customers. You must first, however, master the essential elements of your current job and give extra effort to those activities and behaviors that have the highest potential for visibility, credibility and success. This type of self-management creates the opportunity for you to get to do the things you would like to do and gain valuable experiences, while at the same time assessing if this is a long-term career fit. To do so successfully, master these six key areas of your brand:

1. Personality
   a. You have a positive reputation, conduct, attitude and behavior.
   b. You are invited into key leadership meetings.
   c. You ask powerful thought-provoking questions.

2. People
   a. You display strong social skills and the ability to connect with just about anyone.
   b. You help others be successful, learning from others.
   c. You don't impose personal opinions, but learn to integrate.

3. Policies
   a. You are clear on the written rules for performance success.
   b. You learn to appropriately apply policies to work situations.

4. Politics
   a. You are capable of obtaining buy-in and support of others.
   b. You are able to work within systems.
   c. You successfully navigate the spoken and unspoken rules of engagement.

5. Performance
   a. You bring innovation and identify solutions to business challenges.
   b. You are self-motivated, consistently exceeding expectations.
   c. You align your brand with the direction of the organization.

6. Productivity
   a. You measure and report on your successes frequently.
   b. You keep your word, holding yourself accountable
   c. You maintain a desirable and marketable skillset.

Occasionally, a brand experiences a setback such as Martha Stewart did when she was convicted of charges related to insider trading. However, a branding challenge doesn't negate your obligation to continue to manage your brand. At this juncture in Martha's brand management, "politics" and "performance" had to take center stage. She needed to learn how to work within the system to ensure the best possible outcome for her brand and she needed a command performance before the public eye and her audience, who would determine whether they would continue to support her brand. Here's a Time Magazine report of how the management of her brand brought her long-term sustainability and profitability:

"In December of 2002, while her trial was ongoing, TIME noted that, despite the fact that her usual holiday-time media presence had been all but erased, her line of K Mart products was doing well. In addition, ad sales were up for her magazine, Living, and

her line of interior paint was growing. And that trend continued. Though stock in her company, Martha Stewart Living Omnimedia, tanked during her trial, it recovered while she was in the big house. Within months of her release, she had lined up two new TV shows: a spin-off of Donald Trump's The Apprentice and a daytime talk show called Martha. With the public's backing, she was restored to her status as both revered domestic guru and billionaire."

Though in Martha's words, she "lost a fortune" in her brand setback, and sold Martha Stewart Living Omnimedia for a fraction of its original worth, she is persistent in her determination to keep moving forward. You know you have successfully managed your brand when you survive challenging times. Suffering some loss is expected, however, focus your brand recovery actions by giving extra effort to those activities that have the highest potential to boost visibility, credibility and success.

"Getting over those unexpected hurdles may not be exactly enjoyable, but ultimately I believe that such challenges and the solutions we find give us more confidence. They teach us with common sense and determination we can turn what looks like a disaster into a triumph."

Martha Stewart

Be a Proactive Partner with Your Organization

Can Your Job Teach You Everything You Need to Know About Success?

I have met a number of people who have a passion to start their own businesses and the first thing I help them assess is the degree to which they have learned about business from the companies they've worked for. Nothing can help you become more prepared for becoming an entrepreneur or business owner than the experiences gained from someone else's successes and mistakes.

> "Success is not measured by what you accomplish, but by the opposition you have encountered, and the courage with which you have maintained the struggle against overwhelming odds."
>
> **Orison Swett Marden, author**

There is no level of education, mentoring or coaching that can teach you how to be successful like real experience. When you partner with your organization, you gain valuable insights into their brand and what makes them successful. You can learn how to think at higher, more strategic levels while also sharpening your talent for managing details. Most importantly, you can learn what strategies to employ when faced with overwhelming odds.

Read the strategic plan, the finance report, and other monthly, quarterly and annual reports. Ask questions until you understand the answers and how they apply to your job. Look for that alignment between your job, the organization and your career. You'll be surprised by exactly how much you have in common.

Manage Your Scalability

Position yourself for long-term career sustainability by training others to expect consistently high performance from you as a resourceful performer. Resourceful performers can successfully navigate challenging situations and make things happen by recognizing "opportunity" when faced with adversity and challenges. These performers generate tremendous confidence in their decision-making ability and accountability for innovating on their own.

Leaders look for solutions to their most pressing challenges from those closest to the situation. For sustainability, seek solutions to business challenges and get in the habit of offering the diversity of your thought to help resolve challenges.

Recognize the Barriers to Scalability

Getting laid off, downsized, marginalized, demoted or cut from the team is the last thing we expect or desire but it does happen. Without a clear understanding of the strengths of your brand, scalability becomes problematic. The purpose of this book is to help you design a customized working strategy for your future.

If you allow yourself to get dusty, rusty and outdated serving inside a growing organization, does the liability rest with your employer or with you? There are no excuses for not maintaining a polished brand. Avoid these barriers to scalability by making the proper investment in your brand:

- **Misguided Expectations About Professional and/or Career Longevity.** Mentors share their experiences for us to learn from them, not to necessarily follow in their footsteps. Take what is valuable and throw away what is not, but stay on your own path.
- **Isolation.** The moment your circle of friends, confidantes, mentors, coaches and trusted advisors shrinks or disappears, you are at risk of making decisions that are either not healthy or productive for where you want to go. Surround yourself with supportive people willing to tell you the truth in love.
- **Believing Your Own Press.** Lacking self-awareness. It is humbling to have a healthy dose of balance and reality about our brand's strengths and also its

opportunities for improvement.

- **Lack of Focus.** Rule of thumb is no more than three goals at a time. Too many goals and you lose focus quickly. Get in the habit of prioritizing your day and your week will be full of accomplishments.

- **Poor Health**. When you don't feel good, you don't look good nor do you perform at your best. Maintain proper health and dental hygiene for a truly sustainable personal brand.

- **Lack of Being Financially Savvy.** In the non-profit world we use the phrase "no mission, no money". Conversely, for our careers, "no money, no mission". Entrepreneur Jim Rohn sums it up perfectly, "Poor people have big TV's. Rich people have big libraries." What are you investing in?

- **Lack of Mental Clarity.** Studies show that a proper diet supported by exercise and adequate rest boosts our health and our mental wellbeing. Get plenty of rest, drink more water than any other beverage, take breaks throughout the day, take vacations during the year, get exercise, stimulate your brain, and eat right.

- **Superman or Superwoman Syndrome.** Learn to throw the "off switch" and realize you can't do everything yourself and you certainly can't do it all in one day.

- **Not Investing in Yourself.** If you see gaps in your talent makeup, invest in what it takes to bridge the gap. Coursework, mentors, coaching, training, development, reading, teaching, speaking, certifications, certificates, etc. are ways in which we build skill sets and strengthen our talent. How are you investing in yourself?

- **Fall from Grace.** Lance Armstrong, Lindsay Lohan, OJ Simpson, Mike Tyson, Phil Spector, Tonya Harding, and so many others had the talent but they tripped up. We have all made mistakes. But as noted leadership author, John C. Maxwell states:

> *"A man must be big enough to admit his mistakes, smart enough to profit from them, and strong enough to correct them."*

John C. Maxwell

A brand that is credible, relevant, memorable, likable and extendable is a scalable brand. While you're looking ahead, stop and master the moment.

My husband sent me a card with these words on the front that I keep on my desk. It is a reminder that as much as I strive for success, to stop and enjoy what is around me. If I master the moment, making adjustments along the way, I will have the career, the life I desire.

Continually Improve Your Brand

Ultimate brand management and scalability require a process of continual brand improvement. Evaluation of the relevance, usability and likeability of our talent to decision-makers is how we determine if we are getting the full market value of our brand. Brand improvement includes every aspect of the impact and impression you make on a daily basis. Therefore, at least every six months, conduct a self-evaluation asking these questions:

Foundation
- Am I following My Brand Plan?
- Am I doing what I need to do next?
- Have I established baseline measures?

Motivation
- Do I really want to do this - am I still motivated?
- Am I motivated to do more or willing to change my career path?

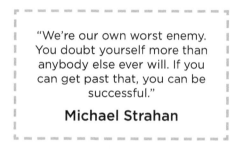

"We're our own worst enemy. You doubt yourself more than anybody else ever will. If you can get past that, you can be successful."

Michael Strahan

Development
- Am I learning and growing at a pace that enables me to deliver successful outcomes?

Achievement
- Am I finding success?
- Am I willing and able to make the shifts needed in my conduct, attitude and/or behavior for optimal success?

Way Forward
- Am I satisfied with the pace and progress of my career?
- Are decision-makers satisfied with my performance and progress?
- Is this the right organizational fit for someone with my talent?

Focus the management of your brand on continual self-development because as market needs change, so will the demand for your talent. Keeping up with the pace of change – making needed adjustments along the way – will lead to a scalable brand such that people see you the way you want to be seen, so that ultimately you get to do the things you want to do.

Finally, remember that some of the most successful and influential sports, entertainment, business and arts brands have refused to allow other people or life's circumstances to stand in their way and neither should you:

- Magic Johnson was diagnosed with AIDS
- Surfer Bethany Hamilton's arm was bitten off by a shark
- Author Stephen King's first novel was rejected 30 times
- Mogul Jay-Z couldn't get a record deal
- Actress Marlee Matlin has been deaf since 18 months old
- Jim Carrey was once homeless
- Henry Ford went broke five times before launching Ford Motor Company
- Bill Gates' first business failed
- Walt Disney was fired as an Editor and bankrupted several businesses before building his Disney empire
- J.K. Rowling was a single mother living on welfare before writing the first book in the Harry Potter Series. It was only after 12 rejections that she sold her first book for $4000 – now she is one of the wealthiest people in Britain!

Don't allow fear, setbacks, self-doubt and other people's opinions to keep you from experiencing all that your career can bring. *Think Like A Brand*, overcome obstacles, establish your Brand Plan and experience your ideal future.

"If you are waking up with the sensation that there has got to be more in life... then there is."

Steve Harvey

Chapter Summary

How do you "Sara Blakely" your brand?

1. **Learn the Culture.** Learn how the work gets done, who is rewarded, who gets reprimanded and why, and the related systems of assessment. Understanding how decisions are made and who the key decision-makers are will also help you successfully navigate the culture. Then you will get to decide: Is this the type of culture where I will find professional success or is it a stepping-stone to other things?

2. **Engineer The Use of Your Brand.** Brand engineering is planning how you want to be perceived and engaged by decision-makers, peers and customers. You must first, however, master the basic elements of your current job and give extra effort to those activities and behaviors that have the highest potential for visibility, credibility and success, namely:

   Personality, People, Policies, Politics, Performance and Productivity.

3. **Be a Proactive Partner with Your Organization.** Is it possible that real world experience can teach you how to be successful more than education, mentoring or

coaching experience? Those who watched Sara Blakely balance her day job with her afterhours pursuit of a new product for women witnessed a woman willing to support another's vision while also pursuing her own. Sara was able to gain valuable insights into her employer's success and leverage them for her own.

4. **Manage Your Scalability.** One important lesson we learn from Sara is how to position ourselves for long-term career sustainability by training others to expect to receive consistently high performance from our brands. Sara's ability to navigate many challenging situations is to be admired and is what we credit with the sustainability of the Sara Blakely brand.

5. **Recognize the Barriers to Scalability.** "Getting over those unexpected hurdles may not be exactly enjoyable, but ultimately I believe that such challenges and the solutions we find give us more confidence. They teach us with common sense and determination we can turn what looks like a disaster into a triumph." Martha Stewart

6. **Continual Brand Improvement.** At least every six months, evaluate the relevance, usability and likeability of your talent to decision-makers to determine if you are getting the full market value of your brand.

Every step of Sara's journey required her continued focus and willingness to re-calibrate along the way:

- Her mission, vision and strategy were focused and well aligned.
- She benefited from a keen understanding of her organization's brand, needs and priorities.
- She invested in her product's brand research while also making discoveries about herself as an entrepreneur and brand.
- She shaped her brand template to ensure her personal brand was positively reflective of her product brand.
- Sara's background and experience in communication shaped her strategy for brand visibility from the moment she began pitching her idea concept to manufacturers until her first sale to Neiman Marcus. Sara didn't see rejection as a failure but instead as an opportunity to strengthen her message.
- Sara's talent adjacencies in the communications and sales fields help to boost her confidence and her strategic plan. None of her talent was lost in the process, even her comedic experiences played a role in the brand's name.
- Sara Blakely's personal brand is scalable not because of money, but because she learned how to accept that failure isn't fatal, to believe in herself enough to invest in herself, to move beyond the place of comfort and to take risks to achieve her goals. Today, this billion-dollar woman is still redefining success.

What do all of our sports, entertainment, business and arts brands have in common? What have they all done that knits them together as an emblem for personal brand development that would boost their market value, increase their career options and create professional longevity:

√   They recognized they had something to offer.
√   Would not allow failure and roadblocks to get in their way.
√   Were relentless in their pursuit of their dreams.
√   Eager to break with conformity and try something new, unique, different, better.
√   Never allowed themselves to become complacent.
√   Invested in their development.
√   Willing to take risks.

You can create a customized path to career success simply by focusing your efforts and attention on the development of your personal brand. I've laid the foundation through the 7-Step Strategic Brand PlanTM, now it is up to you to make the time to invest in you. In this way, you will discover that not only can you *Think Like A Brand*, but you can act like one too.

Think Like A Brand Q&A

I have a boss who simply refuses to allow me to do things outside of my scope of work, what do I do?

Are you bringing your "A" game? If you are not performing at least at a commendable level or higher in your regular duties, then perhaps that is where you start.

If you are an above average employee, then have a conversation with your boss and get a clear understanding of his or her position. It could be it is not personal towards you, but that he/she is concerned that if they allow you some freedoms they'll be asked by others.

Make your case less personal and more about business. How can the business benefit from your expanded experiences? Point to others who are similarly situated to you in the organization as proof that it can work. Identify measurable outcomes with a timeframe and call it a "pilot" so a resistant boss feels in control and able to yank the "pilot" if needed.

If all else fails, look for brand developing opportunities outside of work, either in volunteer or part-time positions until you're ready to move on to another opportunity.

I'm trying to learn details about the organization to gain insights into their sustainability and strategic direction, but everything seems hidden and secretive. I'm afraid if I keep asking, I could be viewed negatively.

Many organizations post information to employee intranet sites where this kind of information is made available to their staff. If, at a minimum, your goals are not tied to the strategic direction of the organization, and this information is not readily available to even employees, even when asked, then there may be a reason to be concerned.

Determine if trusted colleagues have insights and make sure decision-makers see you as someone to be trusted. If you've not disclosed why you are in need of the information, organizations that are confidentially examining their strategic direction could find your request suspect. Your simple explanation that you're looking to align your brand with theirs could put key stakeholder's minds at ease.

If you work for a publicly traded company, financial and annual reports are public and can be obtained from SEC's Edgar filings. If you are working for a non-profit organization, you can also find information through an internet search on sites such as GuideStar and Foundation Center.

How do I go about building my brand without making my boss and other decision-makers jealous or intimidated?

You might not be able to eliminate jealousy or intimidation, but you certainly can learn how to address it by:

Not taking it personal or getting defensive. Try to put yourself in their position. I had what seemed like a succession of jealous and intimidated bosses who appeared to try and make my life miserable by marginalizing me at every turn. Once I put myself in their shoes, I still didn't like it, but I understood their perspective – they felt they should have been doing what I was doing, and I beat them to it. It honestly helped me have a little more compassion for the time we worked together.

Look for allies at their level. Individuals who find you credible, capable and competent and who are supportive publicly.

Be aware of your messaging. Try to pull them in when possible, include them in key discussions. Seek their insights and input, even if it isn't useful. This strategy has the effect of turning your adversaries into allies.

I'm well respected by customers, peers, vendors and most higher-ups. I get offered opportunities and experiences that most of my peers seem to envy, and relationships are starting to strain. Do I back away from career advancing opportunities just to retain the relationships?

The short answer is "no". I love this quote, and it is worth repeating, "When you buy other people's opinion you buy their lifestyle." Embrace this season of opportunity, continue to be open and manage these relationships, and if you can, look for ways to bring them along. Pull back the curtain and be willing to share insights; they either take it or leave it, but you keep moving forward.

I'm building my brand in very unique ways and generating some additional income part-time doing so. However, my employer said it is a conflict of interest and tells me to stop, quit or get fired. I know it has nothing to do with conflict of interest, I've researched the policies. What do I do?

Does the employer have a better offer to entice you to "stop", such as career growth and development opportunities? If no - What would you miss most? The unique brand building opportunities or your full-time job? If your unique opportunities, then make sure you have resources saved up that support you long-term because if you continue, your employer may just live up to their promise to fire you.

I'm a vocalist, and I also love to act. Right now I'm working at a popular restaurant until I'm able to make it in the industry. I've been given this chance to get on a popular television program; I have only one shot, and I'm not sure how to really leverage the opportunity. What are your thoughts?

You're about to expose millions of people to your brand. What do you want them to remember most? You have two audiences: decision-makers in the entertainment industry who can invest in your brand and millions of potential new fans who will support your brand. Speak to both. Make sure they can find your digital footprint through Instagram, Facebook, Twitter and a Personal Website. Put your best foot forward in all arenas, in every interaction. If you are "voted off" stay visible, keep pursuing your dream and leverage your Brand. As vocalist Jamie Jones, said, "Your number one job is to make the audience fall in love with YOU and they will forgive any flaws in your talent."

I've been to jail. Can I really apply this to my life?

I heard it said once that "change is inevitable, but growth is optional." The short answer is "yes" if you believe you have grown. When you are speaking to potential employers and supporters, focus on your growth, not your past, and follow it up with performance. Make sure any mistakes you make are in the growth stage of your life (when you're learning new skills and behaviors) and are not the result of a step back into your past.

I'm unsure of which career opportunities to realistically consider. How do you decide, is it money, benefits, longevity?

Selectively choose positions that leverage the best of what you have to offer. If the opportunity will fully leverage your talent, is paying you full market value (in money and benefits), and you can align with the organization, then it could be worth pursuing.

I simply don't have time to write a plan, work with a coach, and spend intense effort on building my brand. **Think Like A Brand** *sounds good, but is it realistic?*

What you've just read, *Think Like A Brand*, is my life; it is realistic because I live it. I live it because I saw other people were able to live it. I had a crazy, busy life too, but I made time to build my brand and focus on my goals. One thing I learned about being a brand through aligning with my organization's brand, needs and priorities is this: When we decide there is something we need to do that is vital to our success, we identify the things we need to stop doing in order to do the things of greatest importance and long-term impact. What can you stop doing to that will give volume to your inner voice and give you the courage to start achieving your goals?

I have a really bad reputation. I know this. I want to change, but I just don't know how.

I hope you'll take the time to read this book in its entirety, but remember this,

When you change, everything around you must change.

You control your conduct, your attitude and your behavior (CAB), no one else. Own it from this day forward. Whatever you are doing that contributes to this "bad reputation" you change, permanently, today. Listen to your inner moral compass and stop allowing other people to drag you into bad behavior. Do what you know is right. This may mean disassociating yourself with negative influences, getting counseling or coaching. Smile if you frown, and do the opposite of the bad behavior that people expect. It will take them a minute to accept this "new you" but keep with it, and things will improve. People just need to trust that the transformation is permanent. The moment you revert to old behavior you will have undone all the work leading up to that point.

I could tell you countless true stories of people just like you who were able to make significant shifts in their CAB. They faced resistance to their transformation, yet they persevered. And so can you.

I am the first and only Latino in leadership. We are growing our Hispanic/ Latino customer base, and I recognize this was a factor in my hire, but it seems I was only hired because of my ethnicity. I have other talents that I want to be fully leveraged. How do I do more without it becoming a big deal?

When you are the "first and only" especially in leadership, everything you do seems magnified. Sometimes this feeling can prevent you from bringing your best self to work, but don't let that stop you. Embrace your difference, share useful insights while putting your best foot forward in the other areas of your talent. This is as much a learning experience for them as it is for you. Their experience with you may determine their willingness to bring on other diverse talent.

Build relationships and alliances, and above all get a mentor. Identify someone who is at your level who is also Latino outside of the organization, who can guide your thinking and inform your behavior. It is easy to be hypersensitive when you are the "first and only". Try to control sensitivities and let nothing throw you off your game. You know why you're there, now build your intellectual capital, align your brand with the organization and, if it is a reputable brand, carry it with you to your next opportunity.

I've been going on interviews, seems like more than a dozen, and I'm just not getting the offer. I believe I have a polished brand, but by the end of the interview, I just don't always feel I've nailed it. Any insights?

It is tough to answer this one without more detail, but a dozen interviews isn't quite too many in the type of job market we're in today. However, I wonder if you've been able to differentiate yourself fully as well in the interview as you did on paper? For example, did you convey to the interviewer:

- How your talent is unique, different, better and more desirable than anyone else they could possibly interview?
- Are you successfully linking your past experience to the present opportunity?
- Are you excited about the opportunity, and it shows?
- Did you prepare by researching the company's brand, needs and priorities?
- Are you engaged in the art of active listening? Did you fully and completely answer the questions?
- Are you trying to make a personal and genuine connection with the interviewer?
- On a scale of 1-10 (10 being the highest rating) is your brand showing up as warm and engaging (8-10) or does the interviewer have to check your pulse to see if you're still breathing (0-1)?

We can't blame the interviewer if we haven't done our part to stand out and get them to appreciate our talent. Remember, "Chance favors the prepared mind." Louis Pasteur, French Chemist. Branding is about getting decision-makers to see you as the only candidate that can fill their position. Meaning you should make them want to bring a swift end to their search after meeting with you.

I'm working in a job that appears to be going nowhere, but it does provide me with some level of professional satisfaction. I've been here for about five years, and as much as I try to leverage all of my talent and look for promotional opportunities, they just aren't coming. My background is reflective of someone that has done a little bit of everything and pulling it all together for one job seems pretty impossible. How does someone like me **Think Like A Brand?**

I've seen resumes like yours that leave hiring managers scratching their heads in wonder, "How did they get all these different types of jobs?" Well, congratulations on being able to gain a variety of skills; your personal brand must be a winning brand.

Many of us get on a career track and stay there until retirement, but individuals like you are often tapped on the should for opportunities that may or may not lead "somewhere" but your sense of adventure or willingness to try new things has led you to build a unique skillset. This means you struggle with what the next career move will be, and because your interests may be competing, finding one job to satisfy them all is challenging.

Could it be that one employer will not satisfy your career goals? Can you leverage your most rewarding talents at work while fulfilling others through a part-time paid or volunteer experience?

Because of your incongruent talent portfolio, you may find that you get the greatest sense of career fulfillment through a combination of full-time and part-time experiences. Your next challenge will be to decide which category of your talent will be best served and supported in regular full-time work leaving the other to be pursued during your disposable time.

About the Author

"Success is not the result of spontaneous combustion. You must set yourself on fire."
Reggie Leach, Ice Hockey Player

Pamela J. Green, MBA, SPHR, ACC is a business executive, leadership consultant, executive coach, keynote speaker and published author with more than 25 years of business leadership experience. As the former VP/Chief Membership Officer for the Society for Human Resource Management (SHRM) (the world's largest association for HR professionals), she was responsible for membership revenue and strategies to engage and retain more than 260k human resource business professionals!

Since launching her consultancy in 2012, and now as President and CEO of The HR Coaching Institute, she has been serving as a leadership consultant to global corporations, small businesses, and non-profit organizations and their teams developing strategies that lead to greater productivity, employee satisfaction, commitment, and business results! Clients call Pamela to help them achieve breakthrough performance with their HR Strategies, Leadership Effectiveness, and Professional Careers.

A well-known figure in the HR world, popular keynote speaker, notable business leader and career coach, Pamela has been featured in a multitude of media outlets and radio programs; has a number of books to her credit; is a certified Senior Professional in Human Resources (SPHR), an Associate Certified Coach (ACC), holds a Bachelor's Degree in Business and Human Resources, and a Master's Degree in Business Administration (MBA) from Franklin University in Columbus, Ohio. She spends her spare time serving on a number of community boards and enjoying time with her family.

To connect with Pam, you can follow her on Twitter @pamelajgreen, "Like" her Facebook Page: www.facebook.com/thehrcoachinginstitute, and join her networks through www.pamelajgreen.com!

Works Cited

"Abagnale & Associates." *Abagnale & Associates.* N.p., n.d. Web. 03 Aug. 2015. <http://www.abagnale.com/index2.asp>.

"Building Wealth: A Beginners Guide to Securing Your Financial Future." *Federal Reserve Bank of Dallas.* Community Development Department and the Public Affairs Department, 1 Apr. 2015. Web. 27 June 2015. <http://www.dallasfed.org/microsites/cd/wealth/consumers.html>.

"Frank Abagnale, Jr." *Wikipedia.* Wikimedia Foundation, n.d. Web. 03 Aug. 2015. <https://en.wikipedia.org/wiki/Frank_Abagnale>.

"ILO Global Employment Trends 2010 - Unemployment Reaches Highest Level on Record in 2009." *ILO Global Employment Trends 2010 - Unemployment Reaches Highest Level on Record in 2009.* N.p., 27 Jan. 2010. Web. 26 July 2015. <http://www.ilo.org/manila/info/public/pr/WCMS_124768/lang--en/index.htm.>.

"Jay-Z Quotes for Personal Growth - JullienGordon.com." *JullienGordoncom.* N.p., 08 Jan. 2008. Web. 01 Aug. 2015. <http://julliengordon.com/jay-z-quotes-for-personal-growth>.

"Job Openings and Labor Turnover Summary." *U.S. Bureau of Labor Statistics.* U.S. Bureau of Labor Statistics, 07 July 2015. Web. 22 July 2015. <http://www.bls.gov/news.release/jolts.nr0.htm>.

"Misty Copeland | Biography - American Dancer." *Encyclopedia Britannica Online.* Encyclopedia Britannica, n.d. Web. 29 July 2015. <http://www.britannica.com/biography/Misty-Copeland>.

"MISTY COPELAND." *MISTY COPELAND.* N.p., n.d. Web. 29 July 2015. <http://www.mistycopeland.com/home.html>.

"Taylor Swift." *Taylor Swift.* N.p., 27 Oct. 2014. Web. 30 July 2015. <http://taylorswift.com/about_from_taylor>.

"The Power List: The 50 Most Powerful Entertainers (Nos. 1-25)." *Entertainment Weekly's EW.com.* N.p., 8 Oct. 2010. Web. 19 June 2015.

"They Threw It Away - Self-Destruction and Acting Careers." *The DataLounge.* N.p., 6 Jan. 2014. Web. 04 Aug. 2015. <https://www.datalounge.com/thread/13556983-they-threw-it-away-self-destruction-and-acting-careers>.

"Top Reasons Why You Don't Get The Job: It's Your Fault!" *OI Global Partners*. N.p., 28 Oct. 2014. Web. 06 Aug. 2015. <http://oiglobalpartners.com/top-reasons-why-you-dont-get-the-job-its-your-fault/>.

"Twisted Sister's Dee Snider on Fame and Failure | Where Are They Now? | OWN." *YouTube*. YouTube, 5 Apr. 2015. Web. 05 Aug. 2015. <http://www.youtube.com/watch?v=YFyxZ-oIdqE>.

"Volunteering as a Pathway to Employment Report." *Volunteering as a Pathway to Employment Report*. Corporation for National and Community Service, n.d. Web. 27 June 2015. <http://www.nationalservice.gov/impact-our-nation/research-and-reports/volunteering-pathway-employment-report>.

"Why We Explore." *NASA*. NASA, n.d. Web. 27 July 2015. <https://www.nasa.gov/exploration/whyweexplore/why_we_explore_main.html#.VbZ7PEXffl0>.

Beyoncé Knowles. (2015). The Biography.com website. Retrieved 12:57, Aug 01, 2015, from <http://www.biography.com/people/beyonce-knowles-39230>.

Blakely, Ph.D., Johanna, and Entertainment Goes Global. "Entertainment Goes Global: Mass Culture in a Transforming World." *Entertainment Goes Global: Mass Culture in a Transforming World* (2001): 1-13. <Www.learcenter.org>. The Norman Lear Centertainment, 1 Jan. 2001. Web. 18 June 2015.

Clash, James. "In Pictures: The Greatest Risk They Ever Took." *Forbes*. Forbes Magazine, 1 Jan. 2010. Web. 20 June 2015.

Dezenhall, Eric. "Martha Stewart's Damage Control Win." *The Huffington Post*. TheHuffingtonPost.com, 9 July 2015. Web. 04 Aug. 2015. <http://www.huffingtonpost.com/eric-dezenhall/martha-stewarts-damage-co_b_7752236.html>.

Di Somma, Mark. "When Other Brands Attack: 5 Defensive Moves." *Branding Strategy Insider When Other Brands Attack 5 Defensive Moves Comments*. Branding Strategy Insider, 16 Oct. 2013. Web. 07 July 2015. <http://www.brandingstrategyinsider.com/2013/10/when-other-brands-attack-5-defensive-moves.html#.VZZkTzpVtwd>.

Ede, Sharon. "Surviving Personal Attacks - A Guide for Change Agents." *Cruxcatalyst*. N.p., 11 July 2012. Web. 1 Aug. 2015. <www.cruxcatalyst.com%2F2012%2F07%2F11%2Fsurviving-personal-attacks>.

Fontinelle, Amy. "Budgeting Basics - What Is Budgeting?" *<http://www.investopedia.com/university/budgeting/basics1.asp >*. Investopedia, n.d. Web. 27 June 2015.

Goleman, Daniel. "Why Leaders Need a Triple Focus." *Why Leaders Need a Triple Focus*. N.p., 21 Jan. 2014. Web. 30 July 2015. <http://greatergood.berkeley.edu/article/item/why_leaders_need_a_triple_focus>.

Jeff Bezos. (2015). The Biography.com website. Retrieved 11:35, Jul 29, 2015, from <http://www.biography.com/people/jeff-bezos-9542209>.

Johnson, Vincent Trivett and Robert. "12 Jobs That Will Vanish From The Workforce Completely." *Business Insider*. Business Insider, Inc, 08 Sept. 2011. Web. 29 July 2015. <http://www.businessinsider.com/jobs-that-will-not-exist-in-the-future-2011-8?op=1>.

Kyung Kim, Eun. "Martha Stewart: Prison Time Was 'terrible'" *Today*. N.p., 30 Apr. 2013. Web. 29 June 2015. <http://www.today.com/Fnews/martha-stewart-prison-time-was-terrible-6C9676516>.

Latson, Jennifer. "Martha Stewart Went to Prison 10 Years Ago." *Time*. Time, 8 Oct. 2014. Web. 29 June 2015. <http://time.com/3474918/martha-stewart/>.

Lewis, Maddi. "Community Post: 17 Majestic Beyoncé Quotes That Will Remind You To Be Fierce." *BuzzFeed Community*. N.p., 24 Feb. 2014. Web. 01 Aug. 2015. <http://www.buzzfeed.com/mlew15/17-majestic-beyonca-quotes-that-will-remind-you-t-h0se#.uk7zWL2ZE>.

Michael Strahan. (2015). The Biography.com website. Retrieved 11:05, Jun 29, 2015, from <http://www.biography.com/people/michael-strahan-20962977>.

Miller, Laurie. "2014 State of the Industry Report: Spending on Employee Training Remains a Priority." *2014 State of the Industry Report: Spending on Employee Training Remains a Priority*. The Association for Training and Development, 8 Nov. 2014. Web. 29 July 2015. <https://www.td.org/Publications/Magazines/TD/TD-Archive/2014/11/2014-State-of-the-Industry-Report-Spending-on-Employee-Training-Remains-a-Priority>.

Nguyen, Ph.D., Steve. "Being Attractive Helps Get You Hired." *Workplace Psychology*. N.p., 18 Dec. 2009. Web. 31 July 2015. <http://workplacepsychology.net/2009/12/17/being-attractive-helps-get-you-hired/>.

O'Connor, Clare. "Spanx Inventor Sara Blakely On Hustling Her Way To A Billion-Dollar Business." *Forbes*. Forbes Magazine, 21 Oct. 2014. Web. 30 Aug. 2015. <http://www.forbes.com/sites/clareoconnor/2014/10/21/spanx-inventor-sara-blakely-on-hustling-her-way-to-a-billion-dollar-business/>.

Pagliarini, Robert. "Why Athletes Go Broke: The Myth of the Dumb Jock." *CBSNews*. CBS Interactive, 1 July 2013. Web. 25 July 2015. <http://www.cbsnews.com/news/why-athletes-go-broke-the-myth-of-the-dumb-jock/>.

Quast, Lisa. "Build A Personal Brand, Not Just A Career." *Forbes*. Forbes Magazine, 19 Nov. 2012. Web. 02 July 2015.

Rice, Francesca. "Beyoncé: 20 Quotes From The Most Powerful Celebrity In The World." *Marie Claire*. Marie Claire, 4 Sept. 2014. Web. 01 Aug. 2015. <http://www.marieclaire.co.uk/blogs/545716/bow-down-bitches-15-beyonce-quotes-that-cemented-her-place-as-one-of-the-most-inspiring-women-ever.html#8Wl4DKvDloUzjjbU.99>.

Sanders, Tim. *The Likeability Factor: How to Boost Your L-factor & Achieve Your Life's Dreams*. New York: Crown, 2005. Print.

"State of the Global Workplace." *Gallup.com*. N.p., n.d. Web. 09 July 2015. <http://www.gallup.com/services/178517/state-global-workplace.aspx>.

Stephon, Matt. "Sara Blakely | Biography - American Inventor and Entrepreneur." *Encyclopedia Britannica Online*. Encyclopedia Britannica, n.d. Web. 30 Aug. 2015. <http://www.britannica.com/biography/Sara-Blakely>.

Steve Harvey. (2015). The Biography.com website. Retrieved 11:02, Jun 29, 2015, from <http://www.biography.com/people/steve-harvey-20631517>.

The State of The Global Workplace. Rep. N.p.: Gallup, 2013. Web. 27 July 2015. <http://ihrim.org/Pubonline/Wire/Dec13/GlobalWorkplaceReport_2013.pdf>.

Weber, Lindsey. "Taylor Swift Is the Reigning Queen of Celebrity Social Media." *Vulture*. N.p., 29 Oct. 2014. Web. 1 Aug. 2015. <http://www.vulture.com/2014/10/taylor-swift-queen-of-celebrity-social-media.html>.

Wikipedia. Wikimedia Foundation, n.d. Web. 29 June 2015. <https://en.wikipedia.org/wiki/Martha_Stewart#Early_life>.

CPSIA information can be obtained
at www.ICGtesting.com
Printed in the USA
BVOW10s0541241016
465737BV00003B/6/P